EGAC

N 2010 £4 MILLION – INVESTED IN

LLION – SPENT ON RESCUES 97

/ORKERS WHO ARE VOLUNTEERS

REW MEMBERS 3,000 – THE NUMBER

ATION MANAGERS 139,000+ – THE

235 – THE NUMBER OF LIFEBOAT

ND THE REPUBLIC OF IRELAND 330

FEBOATS 8,713 – THE NUMBER OF

THE NUMBER OF PEOPLE RESCUED

SAVED IN 2010 £39,000 – THE COST

.7 MILLION – THE COST OF A

AT £1,266 – THE ANNUAL COST OF

£53 – THE COST OF A LIFEGUARD'S

IFEGUARD'S FULL WETSUIT 163 –

IFEGUARDS 900 – THE NUMBER OF

MER OF 2011 16,664 – THE NUMBER

JARDS IN 2010 107 – THE NUMBER

2010 £504 – THE ANNUAL COST OF

RAGE NUMBER OF PEOPLE RESCUED

A PAIR OF YELLOW WELLIES

MAYDAY! MAYDAY!

THE HISTORY OF COASTAL RESCUE IN BRITAIN AND IRELAND

KAREN FARRINGTON &
NICK CONSTABLE

First published in 2011 by Collins

HarperCollins*Publishers*
77–85 Fulham Palace Road
London W6 8JB

www.harpercollins.co.uk

13 12 11
9 8 7 6 5 4 3 2 1

A catalogue record for this book is available from the
British Library.

ISBN: 978-0-00-744338-3

Printed and bound in Italy by L.E.G.O. S.p.A.

MIX
Paper from
responsible sources
FSC™ C007454

FSC™ is a non-profit international organisation established to promote the
responsible management of the world's forests. Products carrying the FSC
label are independently certified to assure consumers that they come from
forests that are managed to meet the social, economic and ecological needs
of present and future generations, and other controlled sources.

Find out more about HarperCollins and the environment at
www.harpercollins.co.uk/green

CONTENTS

INTRODUCTION

Outstanding courage is a quality that lingers in the mind and touches the heart. Every year on Armistice Day we recall valiant First World War soldiers who stormed from trenches and met death on the battlefield. Meanwhile those suffering from terminal illness who bear pain with dignity and fortitude behind closed doors show courage of a quiet kind.

Then there are the lifeboat crews, whose bravery in the face of an onslaught from the elements is quite simply breathtaking – and likewise too often unseen. Time after time, in a heartbeat, they steel themselves to head off into the eye of a storm when every other mariner is steering for port. Ordinary men and women thrust themselves into exceptional danger not for money or fame but to save the lives of others. It takes a special kind of person to put the welfare of a stranger above their own. Yet it's been the same story unfolding around Britain and Ireland's coast for three centuries.

In an island nation, perhaps the desire to pull those in peril from the sea is instinctive. Once it was fishermen who manned the oars of their local lifeboat, no doubt feeling a sense of kinship with the sailors struggling to tame a high-masted brig on a rampant swell. The loss of sons, fathers and brothers to the sea was in any event a common occurrence for coastline communities, and that too lent inspiration for those that remained. Today, seaside towns are often no longer the domain of mighty fishing fleets, and the volunteers who man the boats are drawn from all professions. Nor are the ships that now come to grief at sea typically running goods or raw materials from far-flung dominions to the hub of a powerful empire. Although there are SOS calls from freighters and the like, it is the hobby sailor with his leisure craft who is now more likely to fall foul of weather, time and tide.

Opposite: D class inshore lifeboat *John Batson*'s crew investigate a cave in Port St Mary.

No matter who is at risk or what the reason, a call for a lifeboat crew brings an instant response. Atrocious weather is a given, as few emergency calls are made when the sea is calm and the ambient temperature warm. Crew members must drop what they are doing at a moment's notice to report for duty, leaving warm homes and safe offices for the vagaries of a wild sea. Lifeboat men and women are 'can do' in a modern era where the attitude is more often 'let's not'. While all have ample training and excellent equipment, it is nonetheless a major event on every occasion. Each swiftly taken step as they hurry to the boathouse takes them away from the security of family and friends towards an indeterminate outing, possibly littered with unspecified hazards. There's no doubt that those who adopt it are a hardy breed with a proud heritage.

A similar impetus to the one driving today's lifeboat crews was behind the foundation of the organisation back in 1824.

Yorkshire-born Sir William Hillary (1771–1847) was a former royal equerry who married well and, for reasons unknown, accrued England's largest private army, which carried out exercises in the grounds of his stately home in Essex. It was an expensive pastime that left him divorced, almost bankrupt and ultimately living as an 'exile' on the Isle of Man. However, his bizarre military adventures had earned him a baronetcy and, presciently, he chose the motto: 'With courage, nothing is impossible'.

As an Isle of Man resident, Hillary witnessed numerous mighty storms and the ensuing loss of life if unfortunate ships were caught up in them. It was a matter of perpetual concern to him.

On 6 October 1822, when Hillary saw the plight of the Royal Navy cutter *Vigilant,* which ran aground in Douglas Bay, he had the opportunity to intervene. Like many wrecks, it lay comparatively close to the safety of the shore, but at the mercy of immense waves whipped up by high winds there seemed little hope for the crew.

Along with a dozen fishermen Hillary, aged 51, jumped into one of two small rowing boats to help in a rescue attempt. Heaving on the oars, the men headed out to sea in the knowledge they would be swept back in the direction of *Vigilant.* The aim was then to fling heavy cables to the naval vessel and haul it off the rocks that held it fast. For his part, the ship's captain began lightening his load, ditching cannon

Opposite: The RNLI coxswains and helmsmen at the official opening of the lifeboat college in Poole.

and masts into the sea. And, against expectation, the two tiny towing boats succeeded in pulling *Vigilant* free. Fortunately, although it was holed, it remained afloat and was brought back to safety in Douglas Bay.

Hillary felt keenly the triumph of the successful rescue – and the despair that followed when he could not raise a crew to help other ships in distress that night. Finally, when he offered a cash reward, men came forward to man the oars once more and many lives were saved.

However, it was only a matter of weeks later that another rescue, this time mounted for HMS *Racehorse*, saw many of the crew saved but resulted in the deaths of six of the ship's crew and three local

Left: Sir William Hillary, founder of the RNLI.

fishermen who had tried to rescue them. Despite their courage and selfless intentions, Hillary knew that the families of the local men who'd been killed would now live in penury. He set about rallying interest in an organised rescue service through a pamphlet succinctly named: 'An appeal to the British nation on the humanity and policy of forming a national institution for the preservation of lives and property from shipwreck'. He distributed 700 copies to bodies, including the Admiralty and Parliament, that he considered would want a stake in a new rescue service.

It was far from an instant success. But, with the help of London MP Thomas Wilson, interest began to ferment and Hillary finally attracted money and support from wealthy philanthropists. Wilson succeeded in giving the idea political leverage while Hillary continued to press for favours from a network of well-placed titled friends.

On 4 March 1824, the first meeting of the National Institution for the Preservation of Life from Shipwreck was held in London, with the Archbishop of Canterbury in the chair. Its eminent supporters included King George IV, who became a patron, five dukes and prominent politicians including Sir Robert Peel, founder of the police force, and Sir William Wilberforce, noted campaigner against slavery.

Supporters were generous, with donations totalling £10,000 within a year. But there was plenty of work to be done. There were boats and boathouses to buy for coastal communities around the country. (Some towns already had privately run rescue boats.) And the programme of improvement was perpetual.

Always open-minded to innovation, the Institution prided itself on keeping pace with new ideas. In 1881 the self-righting lifeboat was generally agreed to be the best option on offer. However, at the turn of the 20th century, no fewer than 60 non-self-righting lifeboats were in service around the coast. The Institution recognised it was not a case of 'one size fits all', given the different coastal profiles around Britain and Ireland. It became policy to let men from lifeboat stations trial different boats and select the best for their purposes.

Then there was financial support for the crew. As Hillary discovered, a cash incentive helped to rally volunteers, especially in areas where earnings were sparse. It meant that the best men could be selected, rather than the only men.

ON 4 MARCH 1824, THE FIRST MEETING OF THE NATIONAL INSTITUTION FOR THE PRESERVATION OF LIFE FROM SHIPWRECK WAS HELD IN LONDON

There was money too for men's families if they died in service. While the spur to join a lifeboat crew was undoubtedly to save lives, extra income and the promise of welfare payments became a consideration to men all too aware that their families would otherwise be destitute if they, as the breadwinner, perished.

Those who helped launch the lifeboat or provided horses to do so were also given small financial rewards. It became common practice to issue an armband or a brass disc to each of a set number of helpers, who would be paid on its return. Without a control like this an entire village might become involved. Often, residents did so anyway without the hope of a payout at the end. In 1898 a pension scheme was introduced for long-serving lifeboat coxswains, bowmen and signalmen retiring through old age, ill health or accident.

In 1860 the now-renamed RNLI bought barometers for selected lifeboat stations in the belief that accurate weather-forecasting could help prevent loss of life. This followed the *Royal Charter* disaster off Anglesey in October 1859, when more than 450 people drowned. The ship's captain had set sail with no knowledge that a hurricane was imminent.

Extending the initiative in 1882, the Institution furnished fishing boats with barometers at about a third of the retail price. The following year the same terms were offered to masters and owners of coasters under 100 tons. By the end of 1901 more than 4,417 had been supplied. By now the RNLI was independent of government, having been self-financing since 1869.

The RNLI conducted experiments. For example, in 1866 trials were held to determine which wood made the best oars. All crews feared losing their oars during a rescue in heavy seas. One finding of the trials was that those made of Norwegian pine were the most durable. Another was that it was sometimes better for oars to shatter than to be so strong that on hitting the sea floor in the shallows they were likely to remain rigid and capsize the boat. Meanwhile oilskins, sou'westers and boots became standard issue to crew, and each boat had a flask of rum, some tinned food and chocolate or biscuits.

The Institution also became involved in lobbying for the benefit of seafarers. In 1893 it was behind a resolution in the House of Commons that pressed the British government to provide telephones

or telegraphs between all coastguard and signal stations around the UK, or to post offices where there was a shortage of coastguard posts, to improve the response time of lifeboats. Further, it asked for a Royal Commission to consider linking lighthouses and lightships with the shore. The resolution won cross-party support and the communications network was radically improved.

Despite these advances our coastal history has been pockmarked with maritime disasters, a litany of tragic events that have saddened British hearts. The loss of sailors, especially in home waters, is a spur for national mourning. The death of lifeboat crew who have wilfully put themselves in harm's way in an attempt to rescue seafarers who would be otherwise doomed is enough to envelop the nation in grief. Such deaths cast a pall over communities from where the lifeboat men and women have been drawn.

From shore we can only imagine what's gone on in the bleak final moments before death closes in on a crew. Gulping, gasping, searing chest pains and cold, clammy fear surely all play their part as people are pulled under the water or thrown against rocks.

Testimony from one survivor gives us some insight into what it is like to be capsized at sea. On 27 October 1916 the Salcombe lifeboat

Above: Coastal rescue meet, to raise awareness of maritime safety, at Cullercoats Harbour.

William and Emma overturned as it was returning to the harbour, killing 13 out of its 15 crew. In 1917 a local magazine published survivor William Johnson's account of what happened.

> The boat, as a matter of fact, went out splendidly, though a little jumpily, because there was, no doubt about it, a very nasty sea. We had two reefs in the mainsail, a reef in the foresail, and a close-reefed mizzen. We went up around the Prawle, and when we got there we saw the vessel which was in distress – a two-masted schooner. We ventured inshore as far as we dared, and discovered that the crew could almost walk ashore, and were therefore not wanting any help from us. Finding we were not wanted we started to go back to Salcombe, and as there was no recall signal continued on our way.

Conditions at sea had worsened, however, and there was debate among the men about whether or not to risk going over the bar at Salcombe. Wet and cold, the men plumped for the direct route home rather than by a safer but more circuitous route, believing the lifeboat was equal to the task.

> At last our opportunity seemed to come. We took in the sails and put out the drogue, and were in the act of unshipping the mast and getting the oars out for the pull in when a tremendous sea struck and capsized the boat. We clambered on to her bottom but were twice washed off, and each time I managed to grab and help a chum back. The coxswain looked to me and asked me what I thought of our chances and I told him, 'Not much.' Then we were all swept into the sea again, and I remembered nothing until I found myself

on a rock some little distance from the shore, with Eddie
Distin on another a few feet off. The waves broke over
the rock and swished and swirled round it, but somehow I
managed to hold on. Then the rescuers came, and of what
happened subsequently I have only the haziest recollection.
My watch stopped at 11.20 a.m., so that must have been the
time, I suppose, that we were thrown in the water.

The men who died were coxswain Samuel Distin, second coxswain
Peter Foale, his sons Peter and William, Frank Cudd, John Cudd,
Ashley Cook, Thomas Putt, Bert Wood, James Canham, Albert Distin,
James Cove and William Lamble. William's fellow survivor, Eddie
Distin, went on to become coxswain of the new lifeboat which began
service the following year.

Another account given at an inquest reveals the practicalities of
what happened when the Seaham lifeboat *George Elmey* overturned
on 17 November 1962 after rescuing the crew of a stricken coble.
The men who had been fishing were experienced boatmen caught out
in a stormy squall, who summoned the lifeboat by firing a red distress
flare. Within ten minutes the lifeboat arrived but got into difficulties
approaching the harbour after the crew misread the pier lights.
The sole survivor was a 32-year-old miner, Donald Whinfield Burrell.
Donald's brother Gordon and nine-year-old son were among
the dead. This was his testimony.

The lifeboat then slowly tipped over to the port and carried on
until she went right under. We fought our way out from under
the boat. I tried to get hold of my son and did so. I had hold of
one of my son's arms and someone with a yellow oilskin had hold
of my other arm but the sea parted us. When I surfaced I saw

Above: RNLI Brighton
lifeboat is called to a
beached powerboat under
the chalk cliffs of Beachy
Head. The powerboat is
refloated and towed back to
Brighton Marina.

Overleaf: The memorial
sculpture at the RNLI
headquarters in Poole
commemorates all the
lifeboat men who lost their
own lives in order to
save others.

that I was one of eight men clinging on to the lifeboat and one man was swimming towards the lifeboat from the seaward side.

I don't know if he got to the boat: I did not see my son. I was holding on to the propeller shaft and a big man, I don't know who, was lying almost on top of me. My brother was next to him and another man along the same side of the boat. Arthur Brown was somewhere at the bow end. There were two other men clinging on to the other side from me and one swimming, and one man was lying on the keel of the boat. Another big wave came and washed all of us off the boat and I could not then see it. Almost immediately, another wave lifted me back to the boat and there were then three or four of us on the boat, including my brother Gordon.
I got my left arm through a winch hole in the stern and my right arm round the propeller shaft and hung on. The waves were still bursting over the top of us. There was a life-jacket light winking about 30 to 40 yards to the landward side and another further inshore and one man was swimming towards the piers at Seaham Harbour.

I clung on and drifted with the boat, the others must have been washed off with the waves later. I saw some lights just north of the big rock on the Chemical beach and we were only 10 to 15 yards off shore with at least three of us still hanging on. We all shouted but no help came and the boat drifted south. I then heard the mast scraping on the bottom, and the lifeboat was washed ashore on the Chemical beach and I dropped on to the shore. I was washed back and forth, and some chains were wrapped round me. I managed to get out of these and on to the shore and round a big rock.

A sense of the panic and despair he must have felt is all the more powerful for their absence from his description. The lifeboat men who died were John Miller, Fred Gippert, Arthur Brown, Leonard Brown and James Farrington. The fishermen were Gordon Burrell, George Firth, Joseph Kennedy and young David Burrell.

Fortunately, technology has continued its forward march and still re-draws the battle lines against ferocious gales and freak

waves. Once worried friends and neighbours lined cliffs and beaches to watch the unfolding fate of a lifeboat, pulled by oars, isolated in momentous combat against surging seas. The greatest asset the crew had were the years of accumulated seamanship which gave them an against-the-odds chance of achieving their goal.

Today lifeboats possess every known adaptation to speed their journey and keep rescuers and the rescued safe. There is abundant radio contact with the coastguard, who can alert land-based teams to help in shoreline or cliff rescues, and often a helicopter is hovering overhead. Lurking dangers offshore and beneath the waves are charted. There are even helmet cameras to record each rescue as it happens. It is all great news for the lifeboat men and women and their families, but technology tends to keep everyday heroics out of the headlines.

Of course there's more to the lifeboat service than these front-line storm troopers. On numerous beaches lifeguards dispense education about sea safety and head for the water in an instant to haul out those caught in rip currents, ebb tides and squally winds.

Many distressed people turn to the lifeguards for help when they've been attacked by lurking weaver fish that deliver a barbarous sting. A flood rescue team was formed in 2000 that operates both at home and abroad. It came into being after the disastrous flooding that devastated Mozambique, and it was on hand when Cockermouth in Cumbria disappeared under a sheet of water in 2009.

The Royal National Lifeboat Institution is a multi-million pound organisation, yet less than 2 per cent of its total income is from Government sources. Consequently the volunteers who work in RNLI shops, and the grocery shops and newsagents throughout land-bound counties who give shelf-space to a lifeboat-shaped collecting tin all play their part in keeping it buoyant. Then there are the innovators who work on improvements for life-preserving equipment charged with cutting the chances of a death in the line of duty for crew members. Boat-builders exercise care and diligence in making sure each craft is fit for active duty. Warehousemen are responsible for ensuring that each boat is properly equipped and each shop is fully furnished with goods. And let's not forget the paper-pushers who keep the administrative wheels of this giant operation oiled and running freely. It's a charity that engenders immense pride and enormous goodwill on every level.

In the 21st century safety at sea has risen dramatically since the days of sail. The advent and proliferation of lighthouses, decade-by-decade advances in weather forecasting, better built ships and improved communications have all played their part in enhancing the mariner's lot in life. Lifeboats have kept pace with increased know-how and would be barely recognisable to the crews from a bygone age. Yet there's a link between the grizzled fishermen crew of yesteryear and today's lifeboat men and women. The eras are bridged by the same impulse to help when there's no other help at hand, to man a last line of defence on behalf of those beaten down by furious winds and foaming waves. Since it was formed, the RNLI has saved an estimated 140,000 lives, as well as sparing perhaps five times that number the pain of a bereavement. Not everyone who has acted bravely to save a life gets a medal. Not every lifeboat story has a happy ending. But thanks to the resolute responses of the RNLI, the seas are a safer place.

NOT EVERY LIFEBOAT STORY HAS A HAPPY ENDING. BUT THANKS TO THE RESOLUTE RESPONSES OF THE RNLI, THE SEAS ARE A SAFER PLACE

NORTH-EAST

TYNE

The very word 'lifeboat' is imbued with notions of integrity and nobility of purpose. Strange then that, in the beginning in the north-east, there was an unseemly squabble about just who should take the plaudits for its inception.

Essex man Lionel Lukin (1742–1834) is certainly in with a shout for being the originator of the first lifeboat. He designed what he called an 'unimmergible' boat – that is, one that wouldn't sink. Basing his design on a Norwegian boat, he integrated a cork gunwale, watertight buoyancy chambers and a double-skinned keel to create the first designated lifeboat. (Various other workaday boats without modifications were being used to save survivors from offshore shipwrecks at the time.)

In November 1785 Lukin patented his design and was encouraged by the vocal support of the Prince of Wales, later King George IV. To see how his invention performed at sea, he gave it to a pilot at Ramsgate, hoping the experienced seaman would conduct meaningful trials. Alas for him, the craft was never seen again. According to his obituary in *The Gentleman's Magazine*, Lukin later discovered that 'the boat had frequently crossed the channel at times when no other could venture out and it was surmised that, having been detected in illicit traffic, it had been confiscated and destroyed abroad'.

So Lukin built another boat, which he called *Witch* on account of her capacity to sail safely in stormy weather. Once again the boat was 'unsinkable', and it was this unusual concept that caused some excitement at the time. Among those who noted its possibilities was Dr John Sharp, who lived and worked at Bamburgh Castle. There he ran a school and a pharmacy, and offered medical care to a poor and needy population. And his concern for his fellow man extended to seafarers on the notoriously dangerous coast off Bamburgh. He established a rudimentary coastguard service with a horse-mounted beach patrol that looked for vessels in distress on stormy nights. He ensured that a gun was fired from the castle in foggy weather to alert ships' captains to the proximity of land and also kept sturdy chains at the castle for hauling disabled shipping to the shore, 'to be lent gratis to any person who has occasion for them, within 40 or 50 miles along the coast, on giving proper security for their return'.

Above: Trent class lifeboat *George & Mary Webb* with Whitby behind.

At Sharp's request Lukin provided a lifeboat for Bamburgh, an adaptation of a simple Northumberland coble which was presumably instrumental in saving numerous souls. Its builder was in no doubt about the importance of the vessel. When he died in 1834, Lukin's gravestone bore the following inscription: 'This Lionel Lukin was the first who built a Lifeboat and was the original inventor of that principle of safety by which many lives and much property have been preserved from shipwreck.'

Lukin's self-penned epitaph is loaded with considerable bile, initially directed at William Wouldhave (1751–1821), a parish clerk from South Shields, who was likewise credited with innovating lifeboat design.

Wouldhave came to prominence in 1789 – four years after the advent of the unimmergible – in a competition organised by concerned businessmen who had witnessed a major tragedy in the mouth of the Tyne that same year. A vessel, the *Adventurer* from nearby Newcastle-upon-Tyne, ran into difficulties just 300 yards from the shore. Growing crowds watched in horror as crew members who had retreated to the rigging to avoid punishing waves fell one by one to their deaths. Although the onlookers were horrified by the unfolding tragedy, nobody was prepared to put to sea to attempt a rescue. Indeed, to have done so in conventional open boats would almost certainly have been a death sentence.

William Wouldhave was one of many entrants bidding for the two guineas prize money. According to Wouldhave, he was inspired by watching a woman draw water from a well using a wooden dish shaped something like an orange segment. The scoop often swivelled on its fixings but never stayed upside down. He forged a model of his self-righting design in copper, lining the inside with cork. The design was commended for its quality but, to Wouldhave's fury, he was offered only half the prize money after nominally coming second. Ultimately he turned the money down. Pointedly, Wouldhave's tombstone was engraved with the following accolade: 'Inventor of that invaluable blessing to mankind. The Life-boat.'

Meanwhile, to compound the confusion, Henry Greathead (1757–1818) came on the scene. Like Wouldhave, he also entered the lifeboat competition. His suggested design was considered 'useless' by the judging panel, but he was a South Shields shipwright, which lent him considerable advantage in the eyes of the competition organisers.

THE DESIGN WAS COMMENDED FOR ITS QUALITY BUT, TO WOULDHAVE'S FURY, HE WAS OFFERED ONLY HALF THE PRIZE MONEY

Left: A painting of Henry Greathead's boat, *The Original*.

They assembled what was considered to be the best aspects of all the entries, chiefly rooted in the plans submitted by Wouldhave, and gave the spec to Greathead to construct.

The result – ironically known as *The Original* – combined aspects of both Lukin's and Wouldhave's blueprints. Lukin was in no doubt that it was to all intents and purposes his work, and now his ire was directed at Greathead. *The Original* was, Lukin insisted, 'to all the essential principles of safety precisely according to my Patent and differed from it in no considerable respect except the curved keel which contributes nothing to the general principles of safety but renders it unfit for a sailing boat'.

Despite a flurry of letters at the beginning of the 19th century focusing on the competing claims of lifeboat designers, it is now Greathead, something of an also-ran at the time, who is generally remembered as the creator of the lifeboat, and this assertion was duly recorded on his headstone too.

It must have caused both Lukin and Wouldhave some discomfort to watch as Greathead was awarded hundreds of pounds by public bodies in gratitude for his work. For his part, Greathead was an accomplished public relations campaigner. The National Maritime Museum has two lifeboat models, made by Greathead and furnished with brass plaques to say so, which were presented to interested bodies. The inscriptions unequivocally declare that Greathead is the designer of the lifeboat. Soon he was richly rewarded by Parliament, Trinity House and Lloyd's of London. He was even presented with a gold medal by the Society of Arts and, more surprisingly, a diamond ring by the Emperor of Russia.

After 1790 Greathead was not only networking but also building boats, and more than 30 went into service around the coast. There was no RNLI in existence at the time and even regional organisations were a rarity. Lifeboat services operated on a parochial level with crews drawn from those of local fishing boats. These independent groups either bought or were given lifeboats built along the same lines as *The Original*. Without wishing to detract from the purity of purpose among the many, there were certainly a few whose main interest lay in salvage rights to wrecked vessels.

Detractors of *The Original* thought her cumbersome, and they had a point. At 30 feet long, 10 feet wide and with a draft of 3 feet, she was propelled by ten oars and had no rudder, being steered by a sweep

Overleaf: Built in 1802 and with 78 years of service to her name, *Zetland* is the only Original class boat still in existence.

oar, so she wasn't easy to sail. If water swept in over the boat sides it had to be bailed out by hand. The main problem lay in the fact that the lifeboats were needed for rescues close to shore. Only the wrecks that were spotted could be helped. For ships that got into difficulties further from the coast, especially at night, there was little hope. Eventually it was *The Original*'s immense weight, which made beach launches so arduous, that hastened its demise.

For this was an era before slipways. Even harbours were few and far between around the coast. Most lifeboat launches took place on beaches, both shingle and sandy. Even with a wheeled carriage to bear the weight of the lifeboat, a launch still required the combined strength of men, women and children from the locality. Sometimes, especially in rural areas, horses were employed to haul the lifeboat into the shallows.

When seas were mountainous it made sense to move the boat overland to the nearest point to the wreck, rather than exhaust its crew by rowing there. Once again a carriage, horses and the pushing power of local people came to the fore. No one knew better than those in seaside communities the weight and bulk of *The Original*.

Astonishingly there is still one Original class boat in existence. *Zetland* was built in 1802 and dispatched to Redcar, Yorkshire, on 7 October that year. Adding insult to injury as far as Lukin and Wouldhave were concerned, an account of *Zetland's* welcome reveals just how Greathead was now nationally revered.
'In the evening the fishermen were regaled with ale to drink success to the boat and the health of the builder.'

Within two months *Zetland* was at sea after two brigs foundered, notching up the first 15 of more than 500 'lives saved'.

At the time Redcar was a tiny place with barely sufficient population to man a lifeboat. But the villagers had pledged that there would never be a shortage of hands, and able men and growing boys turned out in vile conditions, proving as good as their word. When a stricken vessel was spotted a young boy went around the few streets of the village banging a drum to 'Come along, brave boys, come along'.

Initially the lifeboat was managed by a local committee, but their role was soon taken over by the Tees Bay Lifeboat Society. The Tyne being a hub of industry at the time, ships were charged for using it, and

lifeboats for both sides of the river were financed out of the fees. Scores of ships became casualties in the face of a fierce North Sea storm.

On 13 August 1829, the brig *Aurora*, packed with coal hewn from the pits of the north-east, foundered off the coast. When a lifeboat from Seaton Carew failed to reach the crippled ship after three frantic hours of oar-tugging, *Zetland* was moved up the coast for launching. Under the command of coastguard lieutenant Richard Elsworthy Pym, *Zetland* went to sea with a double crew of 26 men to provide the extra pulling power needed to surmount the waves. It was still a struggle to make headway, but *Zetland* eventually brought the captain, his wife and eight crew to safety. The seas were so violent that the lifeboat men lashed their passengers to the seats to prevent them from being washed away. For his part in the rescue, Lt Pym was awarded the gold medal of the National Institution for the Preservation of Life from Shipwreck.

There were also dark moments in *Zetland*'s history. On Christmas Day in 1836 a crewman was washed from the open lifeboat as the Redcar men tried and failed to save the sailors of the Danish brig *Caroline*. The man, William Guy, was a local pilot who had left a Christmas Day service in order to respond to the lifeboat call.

And there was controversy too after *Zetland* was pensioned off by the RNLI, which had been in charge of the Redcar station since 1858. After it was damaged in 1864, during a rescue which saved the lives of seven sailors from a stricken brig, the RNLI replaced *Zetland* with a new and self-righting lifeboat called *Crossley*. The plan was to dismember the popular *Zetland*, but an angry crowd gathered to prevent the work taking place. Eventually the boat was given to local people, who ran it as a lifeboat alongside the *Crossley*, and subsequently its replacement, the *Burton on Trent*. Lifeboat men complained volubly about both. Such was the rancour that the RNLI considered withdrawing its lifeboat and closing the station in Redcar.

Finally, in 1876, the problem was resolved when a charitable group known as the United Order of Free Gardeners paid for a third lifeboat called *Emma*, built along the same lines as *Zetland* but with some improvements. *Zetland* was maintained and operated separately until its last launch in 1880. By dawn in the teeth of a storm on 28 October that year the Whitby brig *Emmanual Boutcher*

was wrecked off Redcar. Her four-man crew was rescued by the RNLI lifeboat *Burton on Trent*. There were two other rescues that day. During one, the carriage of the lifeboat *Emma* became mired on the beach. In another the *Burton on Trent* was holed as it attempted a rescue for the men of the German barque *Minna*.

So when the schooner *Luna* was driven from offshore rocks to Redcar pier, storm-lashed and helpless having lost anchor and masts, there was no RNLI craft on hand to help. Now *Zetland* was manned for the last time, bringing seven crew to safety. Afterwards her 78-year service came to an end and she was stowed in the empty 'Free Gardeners' lifeboat house after 1907. Decades later *Zetland* was rediscovered and restored.

The Original class was not the only design of lifeboat on hand in the first half of the 19th century. The Norfolk and Suffolk class was favoured

Above: Hartlepool lifeboat crew attending to an injured hand sustained by a member of the yacht crew alongside them.

Overleaf: Redcar lifeboat *Emma* in 1877; like the *Zetland*, but better.

on the east coast, while lifeboats built by William Plenty in Newbury, Berkshire, found favour all over the country.

Britain's north-east was also the home of life-saving heroine Grace Darling (1815–42), although Grace, like the rest of her family, had no connection with the National Institution for the Preservation of Life from Shipwreck, as the RNLI was then known.

Grace Horsley Darling was born in Bamburgh, the seventh of William and Thomasin Darling's nine children. They were brought up on Brownsman Island, where her father was the lighthouse keeper, where the neighbours were gulls and the groceries came from the vegetable plot.

Aged ten, Grace moved to an even more remote location when her father became the keeper of a new lighthouse at Longstone in the Farne Islands. Although the children didn't attend school, William Darling taught them to read and write as well as basic mathematics, history and geography. Grace learned household skills like spinning and knitting from her mother. There were also lessons in how to look after the light upon which sailors depended for successful navigation of the treacherous coastline in heavy weather.

Below left: An original timetable and fare guide for the *Forfarshire*.

Below right: Grace Darling – a Victorian heroine and reluctant celebrity.

From their tall lighthouse the Darlings had a unique view of a changing world. The age of sail had given way to the era of steamships, and more vessels than ever before were ploughing through British waters, signifying improved trade links with Europe, Asia and the Americas.

A year after Queen Victoria came to the throne, Grace Darling's life would change for ever following an extraordinary act of heroism that entered legend.

The drama began when the four-year-old steamship *Forfarshire*, sailing between Hull and Dundee with a cargo of cloth, soap and engineering equipment as well as 60 passengers and crew, showed symptoms of a leaking boiler. Finally the twin engines of the 400-ton ship ground to a halt. It was only 7 September, but already North Sea waves were heading for their autumnal highs. The captain had decided to head for the shelter of the Farne Islands under sail. Before dawn the ship became wedged on Big Harcar, an outlying rock not far from the Longstone lighthouse, before passengers could get to the lifeboats. Within 15 minutes the ship broke in two and, when the stern of the ship was swept away, 48 people went to a watery grave. There seemed little hope of rescue for the remaining passengers, with their position remote and the weather deteriorating.

And they might have all died one by one as they clung to the rock if it had not been for 22-year-old Grace Darling. While it was still dark, Grace spotted the silhouette of the wreck, which was some 600 yards from the lighthouse. She alerted her father and the pair decided to attempt a rescue for the shadowy figures they could discern on the rock face, believing the Bamburgh and North Shields lifeboats too distant to be of help in such high seas.

Together they unlashed their coble, a basic boat commonly found in the north-east and designed to be rowed by three or more oarsmen in such commanding waves, and put to sea.

Given the strength of the tide and the winds, they had to row for a mile to reach the survivors while avoiding serrated rocks. When they finally reached Big Harcar rock, William leapt out to tend to the nine scared and cold survivors, while Grace at both oars fought to keep the boat close to. With William's help a woman whose two dead children lay with her on the rock, an

THERE SEEMED LITTLE HOPE OF RESCUE FOR THE REMAINING PASSENGERS, WITH THEIR POSITION REMOTE AND THE WEATHER DETERIORATING

Right: Crew on Sunderland RNLI's Atlantic 85 lifeboat *Wolseley* have their heads turned by the Tynemouth Severn class lifeboat *Spirit of Northumberland* off Marsden, South Tyneside.

injured man and three others got into the lifeboat and they rowed back to the lighthouse.

William and two of the survivors then set off a second time to collect the four men remaining on the rock, while Grace and her mother tended to the others. The bodies of a ninth man and the two children were left on the rock, where they were retrieved by the Sunderland lifeboat later that morning.

Thanks to Grace and William's monumental efforts nine people were alive. A further nine had escaped to the safety of a ship's lifeboat before the stern of the ship was lost. They were pulled from the water by a Scottish sloop and taken to South Shields. The death toll was more than 40, however, despite their intervention.

Soon tales of Grace Darling's courage spread across Britain and the world. The Victorian passion for melodrama drove interest in the Darlings to extraordinary heights. A clutch of artists turned up at the lighthouse to capture her image for a public hungry for sensation. People sent letters of admiration and gifts large and small. One letter, sent by Queen Victoria, contained a £50 donation.

She was the subject of books and poems. This verse dedicated to her was written by William Wordsworth five years before he became Poet Laureate.

Above: Richard Lewis, who worked tirelessly to secure funding for the RNLI.

> *All night the storm had raged, nor ceased, nor paused,*
> *When, as day broke, the Maid, through misty air,*
> *Espies far off a Wreck, amid the surf,*
> *Beating on one of those disastrous isles –*
> *Half of a Vessel, half – no more; the rest*
> *Had vanished, swallowed up with all that there*
> *Had for the common safety striven in vain,*
> *Or thither thronged for refuge. With quick glance*

Above: The crew of a Redcar Atlantic 75 class lifeboat save a kayaker from drowning after he capsized off the coast of Redcar.

Daughter and Sire through optic-glass discern,
Clinging about the remnant of this Ship,
Creatures – how precious in the Maiden's sight!

Grace was even offered a starring role in a circus, a proposal she swiftly turned down, and there were Grace Darling chocolates produced by the original Cadbury brothers.

She and her father received gold medals from the Royal Humane Society and silver gallantry medals from the National Institution for the Preservation of Life from Shipwreck. (It was an era when the Institution only issued gold medals to gentlemen. Those of lesser birth received reduced honours and sometimes only money.)

Her single act of bravery turned her life upside-down, and there's evidence that she found the relentless attention somewhat wearying. It was a burden she had to endure for a tragically short period, however. Grace died of consumption – the Victorian term for tuberculosis – in 1842.

Grace may not have been a member of the RNLI or its forerunner, but her actions did much to publicise the necessity for lifeboats around English shores and she became emblematic of the service.

Yet it wasn't long before the charitable institution charged with saving lives at sea was suffering a dip in its fortunes. Without ready money the Institution could not buy or maintain boats, and as a result, while rescues were still taking place, it was private craft that were generally used. Lifeboat stations were closing rather than flourishing as annual income plummeted from £10,000 in 1825 to just a few hundred pounds.

It was another tragedy at sea that brought the impending cash crisis into sharp focus. In 1849 twenty of the 24-strong crew of the South Shields lifeboat *Providence* were killed on a call-out to assist a ship crippled offshore on Herd Sands. One mighty wave turned the lifeboat on its end, catapulting the crew into the sails, while a second arriving in short order overturned it entirely.

In a new age of philanthropy that grew to characterise Victorian Britain, the story of the selfless lifeboat men and their sturdy craft battling howling hurricanes and roaring tides under inky skies once again touched a nerve. At the same time a somewhat lax approach towards raising money by the Institution came to light.

In 1850 a group of men formed a new committee to run the Institution with fresh impetus. First Lord of the Admiralty and Tory politician the Duke of Northumberland was at the helm. Prior to assuming the presidency he instituted another lifeboat design competition.

The even more capable hands of Richard Lewis as secretary ensured an altogether brighter future for the Institution, which became known as the RNLI in 1854. A trained barrister, Lewis was in office for 33 years, travelling far and wide to shed light on the work of the RNLI and its chronic need for cash. He achieved extraordinary results, which saw the annual income of the RNLI rising to more than £70,000 during his tenure, from a baseline of just a few hundred.

How did the RNLI spend the influx of money? Chiefly it used it to pay for major capital items like new boats and houses to keep them in. However, there were also smaller items that needed to be financed, including lifejackets. It was in the flush of enthusiasm for life-saving in 1851 that Captain Ross Ward, before he became chief inspector of lifeboats, suggested that all crewmen were given new-style lifejackets. His reasoning was clear. When lifeboats overturned, pitching occupants into the sea, lifejackets brought them quickly to the surface for air and so vastly improved their chances of survival.

Initially there was some resistance among the men of the RNLI. The latest word in lifejackets at the time were those made of canvas with strips of cork sewn to the outside. The sheer bulk of the vests worn under the arms and across the chest made pulling the oars even more arduous. However, the worth of the cork life jacket was amply illustrated in 1861 when it saved the life of a solitary Whitby lifeboat man, the others who drowned having chosen a less bulky alternative.

Disaster struck on 9 February, the kind of day known to most lifeboat crew when prolonged poor weather means the services of the

THE WORTH OF THE CORK LIFEJACKET WAS AMPLY ILLUSTRATED IN 1861 WHEN IT SAVED THE LIFE OF A SOLITARY WHITBY LIFEBOAT MAN

Opposite: Tynemouth Severn class all-weather lifeboat *Spirit of Northumberland*.

lifeboat are called on repeatedly. Morning came dark and dreary to Whitby that day, with an east-north-east gale. Lifeboat men and their families could predict a busy day ahead, but as yet no one knew the challenges in store, all tantalisingly close to the shore. The first rescue came at breakfast time, and by 8.30 a.m. seven crew were taking their places at the oars of a coble. The men were Robert Leadley, John Storr, George Martin, William Tyreman, novice William Dryden, John Dixon and Henry Freeman, flung in at the deep end in his first day as a lifeboat volunteer. Their target was the *John and Ann* of Sunderland, which had run aground near Sandsend.

It was a textbook exercise, but at 10 a.m. the alert sounded once more, this time to assist the schooner *Gamma*, of Newcastle, driven into shore about 400 yards from Whitby's pier. This time the men took to the lifeboat *Lucy*. William Dryden stayed ashore while another seven men took to the oars with those already wet through from their first outing in the coble. Ninety minutes later it was the Prussian barque *Clara* of Memel in trouble, in close proximity to the empty *Gamma*. As the crew were brought to safety, the ship they'd abandoned succumbed to the might of the sea and was smashed to splinters.

Hungry and cold, the lifeboat men nonetheless responded to a further call-out. The brig *Utility* and the schooner *Roe* were being propelled into shore at speed. Again the crews were plucked to safety 'amid the hearty congratulations of the immense concourse of spectators', according to the *Whitby Gazette*. Spectators included wives and children of the lifeboat men.

It was only about noon, and still victims of the storm were being driven into Whitby and its surrounding coastline, reflecting just how busy the sea lanes there were at the time.

Although both the harbourmaster and the lifeboat's coxswain John Storr knew the crew were reaching their limits, it was

Above: Sunderland RNLI lifeboats are called out to assist the crew of a 55ft concrete-hulled yacht that had suffered engine failure. They tow her to the safety of Sunderland Marina.

impossible for them to watch sailors and ships flail helplessly.
For a fourth time the lifeboat headed out to sea, with the men
aboard nourished only with a slug of rum. Catastrophe beckoned,
however, as they had already been fatally weakened by their
exertions. They did not get far. According to the *Whitby Gazette*:
'A tremendous cross sea, passing on each side, caught the boat at
the stern of the vessel, turning her completely over towards the
pier, and threw all her gallant crew into the foaming billows. John
Storr succeeded in getting upon the bottom of the boat, and others
were floating about with their lifebelts on, struggling for their lives.'
John Storr, although on top of the overturned boat, died from the
combined effects of exhaustion and the ocean.

Out of the crowds watching from shore came a man who tied
a rope to his waist and plunged into the sea in a bid to save the
struggling lifeboat crew. Owing to the boiling waves, however, he was
forced to return to shore without a survivor in his grasp. When the
carcass of the lifeboat finally reached the shore it was heaved over
to reveal the bodies of Tyreman and Isaac Dobson. Although they
showed faint signs of life they could not be saved. Rescuer Thomas
Robinson was disabled for life when a hatchet was brought down on
his hand in the frantic efforts to free the men beneath the boat.

Only one man survived the incident. It was Henry Freeman
(1835–1904), the new crew member and the only one to wear a cork
lifejacket, which had been donated by the RNLI. At the time Whitby
lifeboats ran independently of the national organisation. Although the
others were wearing lifejackets, these were old-style models, worn too
low around the body to be of use.

The disaster made widows of ten Whitby women and left 46
children fatherless. An inquest heard later that cork lifejackets might
well have saved the men. Five of the men were buried jointly, watched

by a crowd that spilled out of the church and churchyard.

Nor was the day's work done for the people of Whitby. That evening, as the cries of men marooned on the disabled Brixham brig *Tribune* could be heard from the pier, a lifeboat that hadn't been used since eight men drowned from it almost a decade previously was brought out of retirement. It was a lengthy process, to liberate the old boat from its storage shed and transport it to the beach for launching. With a scratch crew it ultimately made its way to the *Tribune* in darkness to save the crew. The same lifeboat was used the following day to rescue men from a South Shields ship.

Soon after the disaster, the local lifeboat committee asked the RNLI to take over the lifeboat service in Whitby and they agreed, providing a new self-righting lifeboat and lifejackets for all the crew. A fund was organised to help care for the bereaved, raising more than £5,000. It was initiated by the Reverend William Keane, Vicar of Whitby at the time.

In a letter to *The Times* on the day of the disaster, Keane wrote: 'We have had a fearful storm today. Half a mile of our strand is already strewn with seven wrecks. Our new lifeboat, but launched a few months ago, was manned with the finest picked seamen in Whitby. Five times during the day had they braved the furious sea and five times returned with crews from vessels in distress. A sixth ship was driven in behind the pier. The men, all exhausted though they were, again pulled out but before they had gone fifty yards a wave capsized the boat. Then was beheld by several thousand persons, within almost a stone's throw but unable to assist, the fearful agonies of those powerful men buffeted by the fury of the breakers, till one by one twelve of the thirteen sank and only one is saved.'

Afterwards, as Whitby's grief subsided, Henry Freeman became something of a celebrity. For his courage in the rolling surf he was awarded a silver RNLI medal. He was pictured kitted up in the lifejacket by fellow Whitby man and prolific photographer Frank Sutcliffe, and this fine portrait encapsulated both the tragedy and the safety-first message that the RNLI now espoused. Despite this terrible baptism, Freeman, a former brick-maker from Bridlington, continued as a lifeboat man for 40 years, 22 of which were spent as coxswain. During this time he is estimated to have saved 300 lives at sea. He was

involved in numerous rescues, one of which is surely in the category of epic.

On 19 January 1881, a ship was seen struggling outside the surf in Robin Hood's Bay. It was too treacherous to come to shore, nor could the vessel continue its journey safely around the headland. People who saw the plight of the ship alerted the coastguard, but with the local lifeboat needing repairs it was down to the Whitby crew to execute a rescue. Given the atrocious weather conditions it was unlikely the lifeboat *Robert Whitworth* could be safely rowed to the scene. It would, declared Freeman, go eight miles overland before it was launched at Robin Hood's Bay itself.

At any time this would be an immense undertaking, given the hills and the state of the roadways. That day there were blizzard conditions and snow lying several feet deep. Undaunted, the lifeboat crew flanked their boat on its carriage as it was hauled along the Scarborough Road by a team of horses. When the animals began faltering, men armed themselves with shovels to clear the path. As word spread, more Whitby men and farmers along the route joined the effort and men in Robin Hood's Bay began clearing the road in expectation of the lifeboat's arrival. Hedges that lay in their path were uprooted. It took three hours of relentless labour before a posse of 200 reached their destination, to be greeted by the cheers of a hardy crowd. All of this was done without anyone knowing the ship in difficulties was the *Visitor*, a Whitby ship. On this occasion the crew members who had taken to the ship's lifeboat were neighbours of the rescuers.

But another daunting task still lay ahead as the lifeboat had to be lowered down cliffs into the churning sea. It took two attempts and only succeeded after a local man, John Skelton, waded into the water to guide it into a safe channel. By now the men awaiting rescue were numb with cold and the rescuers were exhausted. But when the

Rescue of the fishing vessel *Galwady-Y-Mor*. This is the start of 5.5-hour tow in a force 6 easterly by the Humber lifeboat of the fishing vessel *Galwady Y-Mor* – four times the total weight of the lifeboat.

stranded men were successfully collected and brought back to shore
it was a moment of triumph not just for the lifeboat crew but the
entire community.

Much later Freeman became notorious when he married his dead
wife's widowed sister, breaking the law in doing so.

The unsung heroes of the lifeboats were the women who helped
to launch the lifeboat or retrieve it from the sea. This was not merely a
19th century habit but was still happening in the 1930s. One woman,
Margaret Armstrong of Cresswell, Northumberland, helped in every
launch for almost 50 years – until she was into her seventies. As a girl
in 1876 she ran to Newbiggin coastguard station to pass on a message
about an emergency. At Newbiggin, a rescue would begin with the
words: 'Every man to the boat and every woman to the rope.'

At about the time of Henry Freeman's death there were radical
changes in the lifeboat service afoot. It's unlikely he would have
approved, as certainly many crewmen in the north-east
instinctively did not.

For while the advent of the internal combustion engine
transformed travel by road, there were many doubts about the
appropriateness of its use at sea. To start with, there was the
obvious problem of keeping water out of the mechanism. Stout
casing would be needed if lifeboat engines were not to cut out in
the middle of a rough sea far from home. The casing could not be
airtight, however, as the carburettor needed an air supply for it to
run properly. There were fears of fire. Then there was the perilous
effect that wreckage strewn in the sea might have on a propeller.

Of course, there were many advantages to lifeboats driven by
a motor, not least that they were faster, had a wider range and
greater manoeuvrability, and were also more roomy with the oars
and sails removed.

After trials in the English Channel the first motorised lifeboat, the converted *J. McConnel Hussey*, previously stationed at Folkestone, was dispatched to Tynemouth in May 1905. Concerned for their own welfare, existing lifeboat men flatly refused to board it. They preferred to put their trust in seamanship skills gathered over decades, and in each other, not in some new-fangled invention and the promises of a distant land-lubber in an office.

Opposition to the newcomer threatened to spill over into hostility until a compromise solution was found. Captain Herbert Edgar Burton, of the Royal Engineers, a serving army officer who was the son of an engineering instructor, took responsibility for the new motorised boat, and it functioned alongside the existing oared lifeboat.

It was through actions rather than words that local men were finally convinced of the superiority of the new invention. When SS *Dunelm* was stranded near Blyth, 12 miles north of the Tyne, in January 1913, the old-style Tynemouth lifeboat could not reach the casualty; nor could other boats reliant on oars or sail. One attempt by an oared boat resulted in the death of a man who was swept away by waves, as well as some would-be rescuers needing to be rescued themselves. Despite appalling conditions the motorised boat from Tynemouth, *Henry Vernon* – which had replaced the *J. McConnel Hussey* – reached *Dunelm* with relative ease, albeit the men aboard had finally been rescued shortly beforehand by a small boat from shore. The seas were so tall that the coxswain, Robert Smith, was knocked unconscious by a crashing wave. Nonetheless, Captain Burton and Coxswain Smith were awarded silver RNLI medals, having amply demonstrated the virtues of this new breed of petrol-driven motor at sea.

The following year both men won gold medals for their part in the rescue of the hospital ship *Rohilla*, which broke its back on a reef outside Whitby. The 7,400-ton steamer had been converted into a wartime hospital ship and was evacuating injured soldiers from Dunkirk to Queensferry in Scotland. Aboard there were 224 crew and medical staff as well as five nurses.

For two and a half days six lifeboats – one each from Scarborough, Teesmouth, Tynemouth and Upgang and two from Whitby – made repeated attempts to rescue those aboard.

Opposite: An RAF rescue helicopter flies by in Tynemouth.

One of Whitby's boats was manhandled to the beach nearest to *Rohilla* before being launched. Although the lifeboat was damaged in two places when it was hauled over an eight-foot wall en route, it was thrust into the churning water and brought back 37 people in two trips. But a third expedition was ruled out because of the worsening condition of the boat.

However, it was the only oared lifeboat to reach *Rohilla*. Although the lifeboats from Scarborough and Teesmouth were towed into the vicinity by a steamer, the approach was considered too perilous. Upgang's lifeboat twice tried – and failed – to launch. A frantic attempt to reach survivors across the rocks was also taking place.

Once again the motorised *Henry Vernon* proved its worth. With Coxswain Smith and Captain Burton aboard, it travelled from its boatshouse to Whitby at night in darkness, as required by wartime blackout regulations, and then made a run at the wreck. Its motor enabled it to hold steady at the side of *Rohilla*, continually washed over by waves, while 50 people were rescued. One of the nurses, Mary K. Roberts, had survived the *Titanic* sinking just two years before and later said she had found her experiences on *Rohilla* the more terrifying of the two.

A report in the *Yorkshire Post* described the scene: 'The lifeboat throbbed her way towards the wreck and then, when within 200 yards of *Rohilla*, she turned seawards. A few fathoms beyond she discharged over the boiling sea gallons and gallons of oil. The effect was remarkable; within a few seconds the waves appeared suddenly to be flattened down as by a miracle. In the meantime the lifeboat raced at full speed outside the line of breakers, past the stern of the wreck, and then turned directly to the shore. Guided with splendid skill and courage, she reached the lee of the wreck. Already the effects of the oil were beginning to pass off, and the waves were noticeably higher.'

Ultimately, 83 lives were lost. Thomas Langlands, coxswain of one of the Whitby lifeboats, was also given a gold medal, while silvers were distributed to others, such as bricklayer George Peart, who helped to pull survivors out of the surf.

Coxswain Smith finally retired from the lifeboat crew aged 71, and lived until his eighties. He had frequently been decorated during his service in the RNLI. Likewise, Boer War veteran Burton was

COXSWAIN SMITH FINALLY RETIRED FROM THE LIFEBOAT CREW AGED 71, AND LIVED UNTIL HIS EIGHTIES

Opposite: A helicopter hovers above Mersey class lifeboat *Grace Darling.*

R.N.L.B. GRACE DARLING

promoted to the rank of major and awarded many military distinctions before his death in 1944.

Sadly, an altogether less fortunate tale is attached to the *Henry Vernon*, which was sold to a private buyer in 1936 and renamed *Rohilla* in recognition of its role in the famous rescue. In September 1959 *Rohilla*, on its way back from France with a schoolmaster and five pupils aboard, disappeared – presumably the victim of bad weather. Everyone aboard perished, with only a few of the bodies being washed up on shores in Cornwall and Hampshire.

Whitby had the last pulling lifeboat in service in the RNLI, which was kept until 1957 for rescues within the harbour.

Peter Thomson retired as coxswain of the Whitby lifeboat in 1993, when he was 55. A former trumpeter, he had been on the crew since 1967 and was coxswain for 17 years. His most vivid memories surround the rescue of crew from the Scarborough trawler *Admiral Von Tromp* in thick fog and a heavy swell on 30 September 1976. At the time Thomson was still second coxswain.

It was before dawn and three hours before high tide when the relief lifeboat *William and Mary Durham* ventured towards the trawler as it hugged an underwater reef in high seas. Coxswain Robert Allen radioed the crew of the stricken vessel, asking them to release flares to help the lifeboat pinpoint her position. But as the lifeboat approached the point in the gloom where light had flickered the seas became heavier and a 20-foot wave broke over the boat. Allen withdrew to the calmer waters of the deep, waiting for the tide to rise.

Within an hour the trawler crew radioed to say they were going to abandon ship, so Allen made another approach. This time he dropped anchor and fired lines to the wreck, hoping to make a connection between the two. The trawler men were confined to their cabin for fear of being washed away by ever-increasing waves. And the anchor on the lifeboat began to drag, putting it at the mercy of the rocks alongside the fishing boat.

Once again the lifeboat headed out to sea, to where two trawlers were standing by, from which Allen collected two new anchors and two more line-throwing guns. The lifeboat returned once more to the wreck, the crew confident they were better equipped this time. But they hadn't reckoned on two huge waves that swept over them, injuring two. For the third time Allen pulled away, taking one injured crew man to a trawler so he could be transferred to shore.

As daylight came there were reports that two men had climbed on to the safety of rocks while three more were unaccounted for. Now the inshore lifeboat arrived, which could better approach the shore. Quick-thinking helmsman Richard Robinson drove the inflatable on to a rocky ledge, so his crew could pull a survivor off the rock just before it was hit by a wall of water. Although the water swept the inshore lifeboat (ILB) off the ledge, it was unable to make headway because lifelines previously sent to the trawler fouled its propeller. While one man wrestled to free it, the rest grabbed oars and began to row. With the propeller quickly cleared the ILB motored out of the danger area and into deeper waters. Two trawlermen died in the incident. Coxswain Allen received a silver medal and helmsman Robinson a bronze. Peter Thomson, who was second coxswain, received a 'Thanks of the Institution' on vellum.

Thomson had been coxswain for several years when, on 8 April 1982, the lifeboat *The White Rose of Yorkshire* was negotiating rough seas as she tried to enter Whitby after a rescue. Jeff Morris described what happened in his book *The Story of the Whitby Lifeboats*.

> An exceptionally large wave, estimated at up to 25 feet high, suddenly rose up on the lifeboat's port bow. Coxswain Thomson opened the engines to full power to climb it but, as the lifeboat did so, the wave began to break and the lifeboat on clearing the top corkscrewed to port off the top of the wave and fell heavily down into the following trough, hitting the bottom of it at an angle of 45 degrees. The impact was severe, throwing all the crew violently across the wheelhouse. Lifeboat man Alf Headlam hit the coxswain's seat with such force that it was bent and buckled. He received three fractured ribs. Brian Hodgson broke his arm . . . , Keith Stuart suffered cuts to his face while coxswain Thomson received a severe blow on the head.

Fortunately, Thomson managed to clear the area without further mishap and finally made it into Scarborough, where conditions were marginally better.

On 9 April 1988, Thomson found himself in treacherous shallows washed down with mighty waves as he pulled a survivor from the water after a yacht got into difficulties. It took perseverance and immense seamanship to pull off the rescue, and Thomson was awarded a bronze medal.

When he retired from the RNLI, Thomson became deeply involved with the RNLI Museum at Whitby begun by his father. Then another project came his way when the derelict *William Riley* lifeboat surfaced in Devon. The *William Riley* was built in 1909 and served the stations at Whitby and nearby Upgang for some 30 years. It was the *William Riley* that was lowered into the sea by the Upgang crew during the *Rohilla* rescue, although conditions were too severe that day for it to take part in the rescue. The old boat has been lovingly restored by Thomson and others. 'It has now become my life,' admitted Thomson, who takes it to sea to help raise money for the RNLI. It is, he said, 'an invaluable memorial' to the lifeboat men of ages past. His work helps to endorse Whitby's pedigree, as it is one of the oldest lifeboat stations in the country.

However, Hartlepool to the north also has a history that dates back to the beginning of the 19th century. A service began there in 1802, financed by subscriptions and manned by fishermen. After 1875 it fell within the remit of the RNLI.

In its long history Hartlepool has had five stations. At the moment its single remaining station is home to an all-weather Trent class lifeboat, *Betty Huntbatch*, and an inshore 'B' class boat called *BBC Radio Cleveland*.

The Trent has been in service since 1994 and there are 37 in the RNLI fleet. When its crew of six go aboard, they have to do so from harbours or pontoons as the boats are designed to spend their lives afloat. Meanwhile the 'B' class lifeboats come in two types, the 75 and the 85. The 85 is fitted with radar and VHF direction-finding equipment. In an emergency both types will self-right and can be beached without wrecking the boat's kit.

EAST

Lifeboats were not the only tool of the coastal communities when it came to mounting rescues from stranded shipwrecks. One tried and largely trusted piece of kit was what's known as the Manby mortar. George Manby (1765–1854), a Norfolk man, developed the equipment after witnessing the deaths of more than 200 people when the Royal Navy ship *Snipe* went aground just yards from Great Yarmouth, where he was the master of the barracks. Among the dead were women, children and French prisoners of war.

Much later, Manby recollected: 'On the close of that mournful event I vowed that if Providence spared my life, I would apply myself to discover some means by which not only the sufferers might have been rescued, but similar occurrences prevented in future.'

His aim was to propel a rope to the stricken vessels by firepower. The rope could then be used in several different ways. With the right conditions, it might pull a disabled ship into the beach, as many wrecks at the time happened in sight of the shore. More likely, it could provide a line upon which survivors could haul their way to safety. At first, a small rescue boat was needed in order that this could happen, but soon Manby developed a sling for the purpose that could travel along the rope, known as a breeches buoy.

A simple idea in the first instance, it proved more of a challenge to get the rope from land to ship than Manby himself believed possible. 'I began to despair of success,' he admitted. 'At last procuring a royal mortar better adapted to the purpose I hit upon a better medium of connection between the shot and the line (plaited ox hide), which did not, as all ropes had done before, burn at the discharge, and thus succeeded in effecting the objects for communication.'

The Manby mortar was first used in 1808, when the brig *Elizabeth* became lodged on the seabed off Great Yarmouth. Manby himself was on hand to supervise use of his device and the crew of seven were saved.

Like Greathead, Manby became an accomplished self-publicist in pursuit of financial reward. The following presentation was put before Parliament in 1814 before he was granted a sum of £2,000 for his efforts.

> [A grant] would be rewarding an invention which not only saved the lives of British seamen, but the lives of seamen all over the

Opposite: The tractor of Sheringham Atlantic 85 inshore lifeboat *The Oddfellows* on the beach following the boat's naming ceremony.

world; for it had now become so simple and so easy, that it only required to be known in order to be generally adopted.

Captain Manby had invented three mortars of different sizes; the largest would carry a ball, with a rope attached to it, a quarter of a mile; the second would carry it 300 yards; and the smallest, 100 yards. It was true, indeed, that wrecks did not always take place so near the coast as a quarter of a mile; but when it was considered how large a proportion of them happened much within that distance, the practical utility of the scheme would be equally obvious. The largest of the mortars might be carried by two men, in a hand-barrow; the second more easily; and the third might be transported on a man's back.

Manby himself was in no doubt that his invention was just about priceless. He was sure that, where it was used, '… not a single life has been lost on that part of the coast, where many had annually perished.' Yet, perhaps typically, his claims were hotly contested. Manby was accused of creaming off existing ideas and claiming them as his own. There were rival mortars developed by others that supposedly outshone Manby's contraption.

Ultimately, new technology had the final word on the issue, for it was decided that the future lay in rocket technology rather than mortars. As early as 1827 trials were carried out on the Isle of Wight to settle the case between Manby's mortars and a rocket devised by John Dennett, which would likewise transfer a line to offshore shipping.

Coastguard commander Captain Thomas Brigstock reported that Dennett's rocket was without doubt superior:

> Several of the Lieutenants of the Navy who were present have been accustomed to see the Mortar apparatus used, and are, with myself, and all other persons who witnessed the trial, fully of opinion, that the Rocket apparatus has most decidedly the advantage of Captain Manby's as two men can carry the whole along a rugged beach for miles, and into many situations where the Mortar could not possibly be got at all. The portability added to the few minutes it requires to get the Rocket ready, must be considered a very great

AS EARLY AS 1827 TRIALS WERE CARRIED OUT ON THE ISLE OF WIGHT TO SETTLE THE CASE BETWEEN MANBY'S MORTARS AND A ROCKET DEVISED BY JOHN DENNETT

recommendation; besides the advantage gained at night, by the light from the Rocket, showing those on shore the position of the wreck. And also, nine times out of ten, the whole of the line attached to the Rocket may be immediately recovered, if fired wide of the object, which would enable the parties on shore to have many tries in case of not succeeding in getting the line across the ship; whereas that attached to the shot must be lost, and perhaps all the lines expended, before the shot could be effectively thrown.

It's also true that Dennett, like Brigstock, lived on the Isle of Wight and was perhaps even a neighbour. One wonders whether Brigstock could have been biased in favour of Dennett from the start. Manby, meanwhile, was known for his irascible personality, which had the unfortunate effect of upsetting people almost on sight. Whatever the truth of the matter, Manby's mortars initially proved popular, at least on the east coast, and saved numerous lives. By 1823, 220 lives had

been saved around the coasts of Norfolk and Suffolk but only 19 over the rest of the country. No more than 100 sets were ever introduced around the entire British coast.

Dennett himself was in close competition with Cornishman Henry Trengrouse in development of the Rocket. Then, in 1865, both of their models were superseded, along with Manby's mortar, by a new rocket developed by Captain Edward Boxer. Thereafter, rocket apparatus was very widely used in conjunction with lifeboat rescues; it was stored around the coast and operated by a team that responded to emergency maroons. They hauled the rocket to a point on the shore nearest the wreck.

Meanwhile Manby died penniless in 1854 at the age of 89, bitter that he had never been given a knighthood for his innovation and disappointed that other inventions of his – including a lifeboat – went unrecognised. In later life he turned his home into a memorial to Lord Nelson.

In fact, Manby's blueprint for a lifeboat had been built by James Beeching of Great Yarmouth with some measure of success. But mischievous crew men rocked the prototype boat so violently that it appeared to ship water at a phenomenal rate and was discarded as a contender in lifeboat design.

Above: The H-003 *Hunstanton Flyer* gathering speed. This hovercraft has been in service since 2003.

Opposite: D class inshore lifeboat *George and Muriel* meets with a breaking wave following her naming ceremony in June 2011.

However, Beeching was impressed by what he saw. He had many years of experience as a boat-builder, making numerous craft for smugglers when he was a young man in the south-east. His interest in lifeboats continued, and in 1851 he came up with a model that won the first prize of one hundred guineas offered by Rear-Admiral Algernon Percy, Duke of Northumberland, in an international competition to find the best performing lifeboat.

The Duke offered the generous incentive before he became President of the Institution. When he announced it in October 1850 he listed several areas for improvement. Lifeboats for the new era needed to be self-righting, lighter in construction, so they could be launched or beached more easily, and cheaper to build than current models. Ahead lay the Great Exhibition of 1851, showcasing the nation's talents, at which the models in the contest could be displayed. With such generous prize money on offer, the competition attracted 280 entries from across Britain, Europe and even the USA.

Beeching's winning design was reminiscent of the yawls commonly found on the east coast. With a slightly rounded floor and upright stem and stern posts, she was clinker built and measured 36 feet in length.

Left: Humber group scrambling into action.

Buoyancy was helped by the inclusion of cork lining and chambers of air. Water ballast kept in tanks sealed beneath the floor brought the boat upright if it capsized by redistributing its weight. By tradition one set of oars, stowed on the port side, was white, while the other at starboard was blue. One oar was longer than the others and could be used to steer if the rudder were lost.

The initial design was perpetually modified, not least by James Peake, assistant master shipwright at Woolwich dockyard and a member of the competition judging panel. Two new classes of lifeboat were born from their combined efforts which were typically fast, robust and comparatively roomy.

Almost immediately there was controversy about the inclusion and use of sail. While the experienced east-coast sailors found no difficulty, sail was blamed for lifeboat upsets in Lytham and Rhyl during 1852. The RNLI put it like this:

> Lifeboats have nothing to do with sails and they should be forbidden in most, if not all, cases. The Yarmouth, Lowestoft, Southwold and Deal boatmen are so skilful in the management of their boats that they, perhaps, form an exception; but as a general rule sails should not be allowed in a lifeboat. In making for a beach before a heavy sea it is the common practice with boats on the coasts of Northumberland and Yorkshire when they see a heavy breaker following them, to hold water with their oars or even to back the boat towards it rather than pull from it as in the latter case it is most probable the boat will broach-to and get filled, and even risk being upset. Now if a boat is under sail, she cannot be backed or her way be stopped with safety; and it was in running for the shore under sail that the Rhyl lifeboat was thus caught by a breaker and upset.

The self-righting element of the lifeboat was to most crews an endearing feature. But lifeboat men on the east coast disliked the way self-righters rode high in the water. They preferred the Norfolk and Suffolk class of lifeboat that mimicked their fishing boats in design. Although these boats wouldn't right themselves, they were immensely stable, and under the expert guidance of fishermen the Norfolk and Suffolk lifeboats saved the lives of many throughout the 19th century. But no boat was infallible.

It was a Norfolk and Suffolk class lifeboat at the centre of a disaster at Caister in December 1901. The lifeboat *Beauchamp* struggled to launch through the breakers after a ship washed up on Barber Sands. Among the helpers pushing it out to sea time and again was James Haylett, formerly the assistant coxswain of the Caister lifeboat but by now, aged 78, long retired.

Less than an hour after the *Beauchamp* left the beach, a howl went up from the townspeople gathered on the shore. The lifeboat was cannoning in upside down and no one knew where the missing crewmen were. Helped by one of his grandsons, Haylett plunged into the water to rescue three men, including another grandson, Walter, and his son-in-law Charles Knight. However, the rest of the crew were lost, including two of his sons. Haylett stayed on the beach for 12 hours despite being drenched and cold, showing remarkable endurance for a man of his years. Ironically the fishing smack the lifeboat men had in their sights survived the storm and set sail the following morning, unaware of the disastrous rescue attempt made on its behalf.

Haylett won a gold medal from the RNLI, which was presented to him by King Edward VII at Sandringham just a few weeks afterwards. Later, during a Board of Trade inquiry into the disaster, Haylett was asked whether the crew would have abandoned a search for the lost vessel. 'Caister lifeboat men never turn back,' he declared, and the motto has been attached to the volunteers from the resort ever since. '[They] would have kept there till now if necessary to save men in distress.'

From the same mould came coxswain Sydney James Harris of Gorleston lifeboats, who won a silver medal from the RNLI in recognition of his courage no fewer than five times. In a career spanning 30 years and bridging distinct eras, he was coxswain of three different lifeboats, the oared *Thora Zelma*, the steam lifeboat *James Stevens No. 3* and the motorised *Mark Lane No. 3*. He finally retired in 1921, seven years before his death.

'Sparkes' Harris won the first medal in January 1905 after a strong south-east wind blew into a furious gale. Darkness was falling as the Lowestoft brig *Celerity* got into difficulties four miles out of Gorleston.

Opposite: Sheringham's *Manchester Unity of Oddfellows* is launched from a trailer into rough seas.

Right: Skegness Mersey class lifeboat *Lincolnshire Poacher* is launched from a snowy beach.

The steam lifeboat headed off in freezing conditions to save six crew men. Despite the wintry conditions, the lifeboat bided its time until the early hours in order to return across the Gorleston bar. The lifeboat's chief engineer James Sclanders was similarly rewarded.

Later the same year, when the lugger *Fruitful* was wrecked with eight men aboard, Harris swam to the vessel after two previous attempts to secure a line failed. All were saved.

On 28 October 1909, aboard the self-righting *Mark Lane* lifeboat, Harris put down his anchor and veered towards the wrecked SS *Clunie* from Aberdeen, saving four men who'd been clinging to the rigging. He then pursued the drifting casualty through wreckage-strewn waters before it was brought under tow. His brother, assistant coxswain Ellery Harris, was likewise awarded a silver medal for his part in the rescue.

In 1912 the SS *Egyptian*, loaded with concrete and iron, became stranded off Yarmouth. On the scene, Harris and his men took 13 people to safety, including the master's wife and child. However, 20 more chose to stay aboard. Any hopes they had of saving the 2,923-ton ship in the easterly gale were misplaced, however. Concerned, the lifeboat men went out twice later in the day but failed to find the ship in driving rain. A third outing in the night brought them to the SS *Egyptian* and they found that the 20, now defeated by the conditions, were ready to head for land. Harris floated a bladder to the ship on the end of a rope and, once the rope was secure, the men climbed back across it. Apart from the silver medal Harris received the American Cross of Honor for what was regarded as the 'most heroic life-saving service' during 1912–13.

He won his final medal early in March 1916, when the Jersey schooner *Dart* sank in shallow water off Corton, in Suffolk, in snow and violent high winds. The men aboard had been left clinging to the rigging and were rigid with cold and facing certain death until

the *Mark Lane* approached. Lifeboat crew man Edward Bensley leapt to the *Dart* to transfer the men, who were largely unable to help themselves, and was himself awarded a silver medal.

With characteristically wide beaches washed over by fast-running tides that submerge shifting sandbanks within moments, Britain's east coast can be unexpectedly treacherous for sailors. Nevertheless it always used to be full of shipping, as all trading goods were carried by sea before the age of railways, which began in the middle of the 19th century. Even then, the North Sea trunk route off the east coast remained busy, with most of the vessels small shore-huggers that were vulnerable to wild weather. In just nine years, between 1866 and 1875, an estimated 10,000 commercial ships were lost off the east coast.

On the east coast there were a number of beach companies who offered repair work for passing ships, sought salvage from wrecks and also operated independent lifeboats. Typically using yawls, the type of boats favoured in East Anglia, men would put to sea after being alerted by a system of coastal look-outs. There were also privately run lifeboats operating outside the embrace of beach companies, including one in Sheringham, Norfolk, paid for by a well-to-do local family. The first of the private lifeboats in Sheringham – in reality a slightly modified fishing boat – was built in 1826 and named the *Upcher* after the family that donated the money. There are no records attached to its operation.

It was replaced in 1838 by the *Augusta*, built with timbers hewn from woods near Sheringham and named after Augusta Upcher, who died of tuberculosis aged 20. It is said that the *Augusta* launched more than 200 times and saved 1,000 lives, but again records related to it are sketchy. However, she was in service for more than 50 years before being replaced by the *Henry Ramey Upcher*, which itself was in service between 1894 and 1935. Intriguingly, the RNLI also had a boat in Sheringham after 1867

Above: Humber lifeboat crew assist an injured crew member – who had ruptured a ligament in his knee – from the sail training vessel *Tenacious*.

that operated alongside the *HRU*. Unsurprisingly, there was rivalry, albeit generally friendly in tone, between the private and charitable institutions, which manifested itself in local regattas. The *Henry Ramey Upcher* was never converted with a motor.

Local people who learned the quirks of time and tide on behalf of the beach companies and private lifeboats gradually transferred their skills to the RNLI as the latter proliferated. Priceless knowledge banked over a lifetime came to good use in wartime Britain when young men who might have been expected to volunteer for lifeboat service were instead called up to serve in the nation's army, navy or air force. Older men, who had probably parted company with a life at sea some years before, were driven back into the lifeboats by an urge to fight a common enemy. For them, it was the sea itself.

In September 1918 it was an ageing crew that took to the Lowestoft lifeboat *Kentwell* when the sloop *Pomona* went aground on the Suffolk coast. A north-easterly gale was whipping up 20-foot waves. The operation to rescue the ship's company took five muscle-stretching hours. Four of the crew were aged over 50, a dozen were over 60, and two had accomplished three score years and ten.

It was, of course, the same story all around the British and Irish coast during the First and Second World Wars. But there is no better illustration of just how the experienced older lifeboat crew came into their own during times of conflict than Henry Blogg (1876–1954).

Blogg was born in Cromer and was brought up in a fishing family. Although he was a promising scholar, he left school aged 11 to help on his stepfather's crab boat. With a full seven years of seafaring experience behind him he joined the lifeboat crew in 1894 at the age of 18.

His first emergency was in December that year amid snow, sleet and hail. Atrocious weather didn't put Blogg off, though. After eight years he became second coxswain and then, seven years later, coxswain. At the outbreak of the First World War he was, at 42, already far too old for active service. But he remained with the lifeboat crew and won a gold medal in January 1917 for the heroic rescue of 11 crew men from the SS *Fernebo* after its boiler exploded.

Exhausted from a previous call-out, the Cromer men nonetheless manned the oars of the *Louisa Heartwell*. However, with pounding surf, it was impossible to launch the lifeboat from the beach, despite the vigorous efforts of numerous servicemen stationed in the town. The power of the sea was so great that five of the oars snapped, while a further three were lost.

Undeterred, and still determined to ensure the men of the Swedish ship were rescued, Blogg sent for replacement oars, and finally they fought through the surf to make contact with one section of the shattered ship just before midnight. Eleven men were saved.

A gold medal was awarded to Blogg, for his heroic persistence, and a silver to the second coxswain, William Davies. Another silver medal went to Private Stewart Seaforth, a soldier from the Highlanders who helped on the beach. The remaining dozen men who rowed the lifeboat out of Cromer received bronze medals, the first time these had ever been awarded.

The remaining years of Blogg's RNLI service were strewn with medals. In 1932 he won a silver medal, for his part in the rescue of 29 crew from the Italian ship *Monte Nevoso*, along with a Tyrolean sheepdog who was a passenger and later became his pet. There was another silver medal the following year for what Blogg described as the worst journey he had ever known.

Going to the rescue after a barge went aground, again the lifeboat had difficulty leaving the beach as it was buffeted by winds, but it finally liberated the barge's crew, who were numb with cold and fear. A further silver medal came his way in 1939, just after the outbreak of the Second World War, when he and his crew rescued 29 men from the Greek steamer *Mount Ida*.

Still, Blogg's courage and tenacity were by no means spent. On 5 August 1941, when he was 65 years old, he set his lifeboat into the teeth of a gale to help rescue the men of six convoy ships wrecked on Haisborough Sands. Before the day was out, 88 men had been saved, all having been shuttled from wrecked ship to waiting destroyer. He earned another silver medal that same year, in the same treacherous part of the sea, executing the rescue of 44 from a grounded merchant ship.

In March 1946 Blogg had the opportunity to retire but asked whether he could serve a further year. Consequently it wasn't until he was 71 that he finally quit the RNLI after 53 years.

Above: Francis R Flint's oil painting of the Cromer lifeboat *Henry Blogg*, named after the legendary lifeboat man.

His mantelpiece was further decorated with a George Cross and a British Empire Medal.

Further up the coast at Spurn Point on the Humber lies the only coastal RNLI station to have a full-time paid crew, who live there with their families among the rich bird life some miles from the nearest neighbours. With the area remote and the shipping lanes busy, the Humber team provides a valuable service. It's been home to two of the 20th century's most remarkable lifeboat men.

Coxswain Robert Cross first joined the Spurn crew in 1902, but left to join the crew of a herring boat some years afterwards. In 1909 he went out with the Flamborough lifeboat to help several cobles caught in a gale. Two of them were lost, and his brother and two nephews were among the dead. Afterwards he decided to devote his life to saving lives.

Cross was made coxswain at Spurn two years after the tragedy, when the RNLI took over the running of the Humber lifeboat. A devout Methodist, he served there for 31 years until he retired in

AS HE DROVE AGAINST THE STERN, THE SHIP BEGAN TO ROLL, AND AT LAST THE CAPTAIN WAS ABLE TO JUMP ABOARD.

Opposite: A Humber lifeboat crew – complete with oilskins, sou'westers and kapok lifejackets – in 1900.

1943 at the age of 67. By that time he had accrued two gold, three silver and two bronze medals as well as a George Medal. During the rescues he carried out he saved at least 400 people, including 244 in the war years.

Cross knew better than most how unforgiving the sea off the east coast can be. Yet this was where Humber lifeboat coxswain Brian Bevan, who became legendary for his courage, also knew his finest hours, saving at least 300 lives over the course of his career in uniformly terrible conditions. In a matter of months he earned gold, silver and bronze medals, reflecting his extraordinary conduct.

On New Year's Eve 1978, in sub-freezing temperatures, the coaster *Diana V*, carrying six passengers, was battling high winds and huge swells and taking a battering. She was in a critical condition. *The City of Bradford VI* lifeboat, commanded by Bevan, was their only hope. Skilfully overcoming the treacherous conditions, Bevan manoeuvred the lifeboat three times into a position alongside the vessel and rescued a child, a woman and five men, including the captain, who at one point was feared to have been swept away.

Having received a silver medal for the heroic act, it was not long until he was in action again. In the early hours of 14 February 1979, the 414-ton cargo ship *Revi* was reported to be in distress during a voyage from France to Newcastle. By the time Bevan and his crew had got there, she was listing and taking on huge amounts of water in conditions almost identical to those of the rescue of *Diana V*.

The unpredictable seas meant that it was impossible to judge how they could get close enough without the lifeboat being smashed to pieces by the large tanker, which was being tossed around as if it was a toy in a bath. Bevan acted quickly, dodging in and out from beneath the vessel that was in turns rising above them, then threatening to crash down on him and his crew. Several times he tried and failed to get to a position where the four men on board could leap to safety.

Eventually, he managed to rescue the two crew members and the first mate, which left just the captain. The ship was completely submerged by three giant waves, effectively condemning her to the bottom of the ocean. Yet the captain was still visible, holding on to the rails. It was now or never for Bevan. As he drove against the stern, the ship began to roll, and at last the captain was able to jump aboard. Five minutes later, the ship rolled for the last time and sank to the depths of the icy North Sea. Bevan was awarded a gold medal for gallantry.

Around 24 hours later, the Humber lifeboat went to the aid of Romanian cargo ship *Savinesti,* which had an engine failure and was threatening to run aground. In poor visibility and losing their radar, MF radio and echo sounder to the waves which were pounding their deck, Bevan and his crew were faced with a seemingly impossible task. Thankfully, the storms started to ease and the Humber lifeboat escorted the *Savinesti* to safety. For this Bevan received a bronze medal for gallantry, and all three medals were presented to him in one ceremony.

Curiously Bevan had never learned how to swim, having been thrown into the deep end of a swimming pool as a prank when he was younger. When he retired in 2001 after 35 years' service, he acknowledged that he would at that point have failed one of the RNLI's entry requirements, to swim 100 metres fully clothed.

Bevan's actions catapulted him into the public eye. Young girls would scream for his autograph. He appeared on *This Is Your Life* and even lunched with the Queen. His life would never be the same again. 'I went [to the Humber station] for a quiet life,' he said, 'but after winning the medals I ended up doing lots of media interviews and became quite well known.' He was awarded an MBE in 1999.

Further south are some of Britain's most traditional seaside resorts. Although its popularity with tourists has dimmed, Skegness remains a busy town with visitors drawn to its wide and sandy beaches. But the east coast is also a place of dangerous currents and rip-tides. Accordingly Skegness has two lifeboats to deal with the emergencies that regularly occur off its coasts.

There's no harbour in which to moor a lifeboat, and the gradients are such that a slipway is out of the question. So at Skegness a lifeboat is launched today just as they always have been, transported over the sands on a carriage. Once it was people and horses that helped to propel the carriage. Now the heavy work is done by a tractor.

The Mersey class lifeboat, *Lincolnshire Poacher*, arrived in Skegness in 1990 after £600,000 was raised locally for a new lifeboat and boathouse. At the time the boat represented cutting-edge design.

Right: A Skegness lifeboat, which has been pulled by horses across the sand to the sea.

Built with an aluminium hull and watertight wheelhouse that ensured it would right after a capsize in five seconds, it was light and compact, had a top speed of 16 knots and was furnished with the best in-cab technology available. Lifeboat design has since moved on, however, and like other Mersey class lifeboats it will be replaced by the new Shannon class lifeboat in 2013.

In 2010 Skegness welcomed a new £31,000 'D' class lifeboat. Although rigid inflatable boats (RIBs) like this one were first introduced in 1963, the design has continued to evolve and this is among the most modern. The money for it was raised over a number of years by drinkers at the Peterborough Real Ale festival. Accordingly, the boat is called *Peterborough Beer Festival IV* – and when it was launched it was beer rather than champagne that was poured over its bow.

D class boats are fast, powerful and easy to manoeuvre, which makes them ideal for rescues in surf or close to shore. The 'D' class boat that previously operated out of Skegness, *Leicester Fox II*, was retired to the RNLI training fleet.

Further down the coast, Southend on Sea is also a hive of activity in the summer months. Its lifeboat history has for years been intertwined with that of the pier, one of the longest in Europe. When the coaster *Kingsabbey* ploughed through the pier on 30 June 1986, it left the lifeboat house isolated at one end. There are two D class boats stationed here, alongside a B class boat like that in Hartlepool. In 1989 it was the crew of the D class lifeboat that helped the B class Atlantic model *Percy Garon II* after both its engines failed during a stormy rescue.

Southend also has one of four hovercraft in the RNLI fleet, with the other three stationed at Hunstanton, Morecambe and New Brighton. All locations have acres of shallows and sands or mud-flats similar to Southend. Hovercraft have been used for rescues since 2002. Two large fans mounted on the back provide the thrust

Above: A passenger suffering stomach pains on the liner *Pride of Bruges* is stretchered to safety with his wife onto the Humber Severn class lifeboat and taken to hospital.

necessary to power the vehicle, which is cushioned by air pressure.

It's a far cry from the yawls that were once familiar sights on the coast in this vicinity. However, the Norfolk and Suffolk lifeboats of the past have not disappeared entirely. The *James Stevens No. 14*, a 43-footer, was built in London at Thames Ironworks, like many lifeboats of the era, and launched in 1900. A clunky model, she was too big to launch from the beach, so stayed at moorings off the pier in Walton-on-the-Naze in Essex.

In 1906 she became one of the earliest lifeboats to be converted from sail by the addition of a petrol engine, a 40-horsepower model which gave her a flat-out speed in a fair wind of eight knots. Reflecting early concerns about the reliability of the petrol engine, oars and sails were retained just in case. However, generally the community was more welcoming of the modern interloper than the people of Tynemouth, where the *J. McConnel Hussey* received a rough reception. In her entire 22-year service span the engine only failed three times: once the crankshaft snapped, once it failed to start and once it ran out of fuel, when the boat returned home under sail. Indeed, the *James Stevens No. 14* went on twice as many 'shouts' as other early motorised lifeboats and saved double the number of lives.

Between 1900 and 1928 the *James Stevens No. 14* rescued 227 people, including 92 passengers and crew of SS *Peregrine* of London in December 1917 after it ran aground off Clacton-on-Sea in a force-nine gale. At first, given the terrible weather, it was a challenge simply to find the wreck. Then it took six attempts before the lifeboat could pull alongside the 780-ton ship. In a shuttle by the lifeboat, 59 passengers and the chief steward were taken to a waiting patrol vessel. In a race against time, as the ship was breaking up, the lifeboat returned for the remaining 32 crew members. Coxswain Willie Hammond received a silver medal and

IN A RACE AGAINST TIME, AS THE SHIP WAS BREAKING UP, THE LIFEBOAT RETURNED FOR THE REMAINING 32 CREW MEMBERS

second coxswain John Byford a bronze. The rescue took all night and left the lifeboat badly damaged.

James Stevens No. 14 left service at Walton-on-the-Naze at the same time as Hammond in 1928. Six months before she was replaced, she went almost 40 miles out to sea in a force-nine gale on 22 December 1927 to help SS *Cuthbert*. Although it is a feat often undertaken these days in modern boats, this was a rare and courageous journey for men in an open boat. (The replacement, the *E.M.E.D.*, took part in the rescue of British servicemen at Dunkirk, but was crewed by naval ratings rather than lifeboat men.)

After years spent as a fireboat in the Second World War and then as a houseboat, the *James Stevens No. 14* was discovered and brought back to Walton and Frinton lifeboat station in 1998, not for service but for restoration as the oldest surviving motor lifeboat in the world.

Opposite: Tamar class lifeboat *Lester* is launched in 2008 following her naming ceremony.

Below: Tyne class lifeboat *Ruby and Arthur Reed II* launches in Cromer.

SOUTH

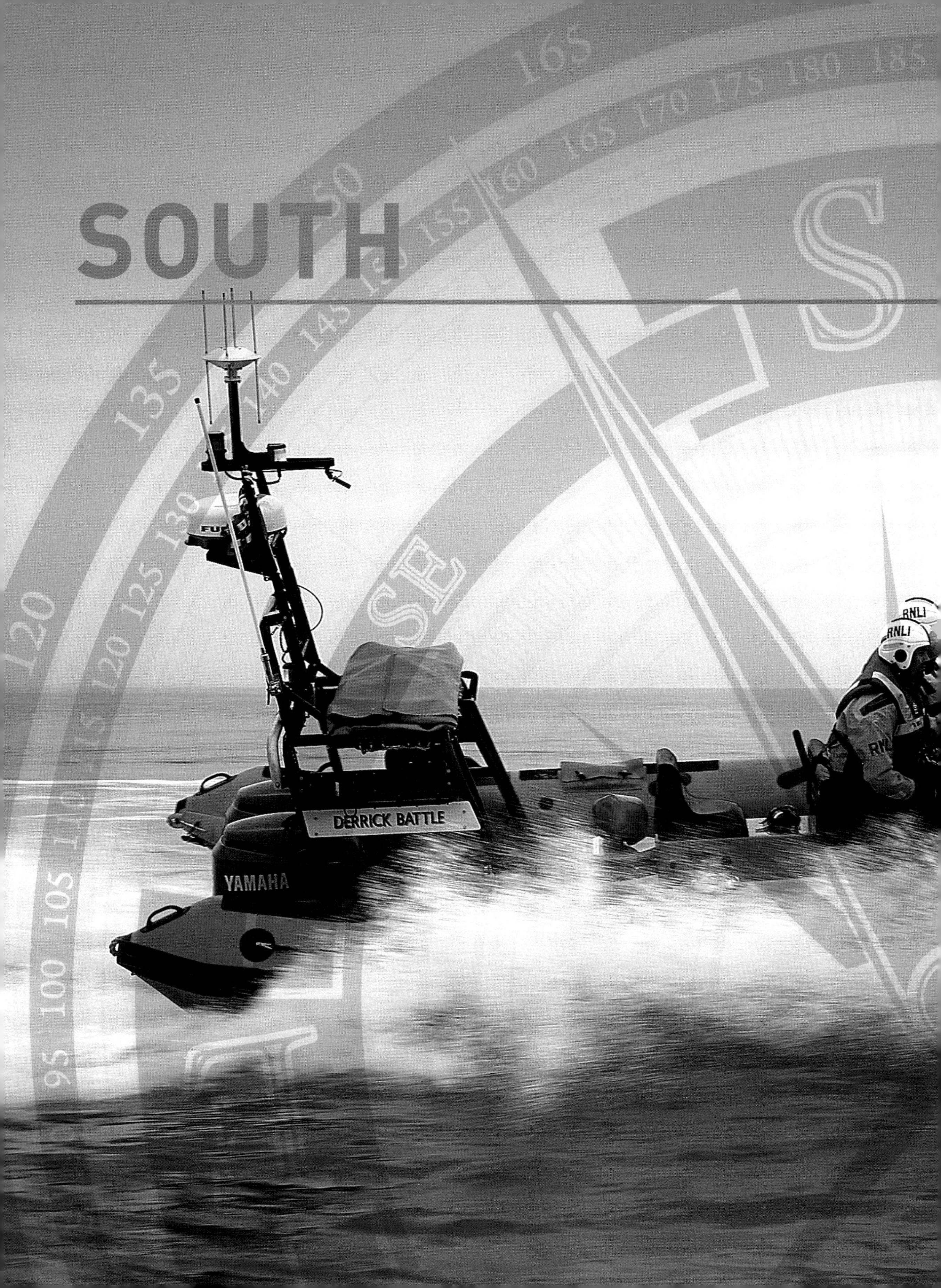

THAMES
DOVER
WIGHT

The shrieking timbers of a Swedish brig announced impending catastrophe for the crew of the *Carl Jean* as it lurched towards the shores of the English Channel in July 1824. With its cargo of Spanish salt and wine shifting ominously in the hold, waves from a heaving sea rose to meet the dipping mast.

From his vantage point ashore, Charles Fremantle, Royal Naval officer and commander of the Lymington coastguard, witnessed the unfolding drama, with the listing ship broadside to the beach. The prospect of fellow sailors dying on his watch was too hard to bear.

With a line fastened to his body he swam from the sands to the awkwardly-angled vessel and climbed aboard. His first thought was to liberate the ship's lifeboats, but these were instantly swamped. He had other ideas but the crew either didn't understand or didn't listen. As the ship continued to creak dangerously, Fremantle had no choice but to head back for shore the same way he had come, ultimately hauled to safety, exhausted.

The ship broke up, as Fremantle knew it would. Fortunately for the crew, they managed to cling to the mainmast, which was then washed into the beach.

For his efforts Fremantle was awarded the first gold medal given by the newly formed National Institution for the Preservation of Life from Shipwrecks. This is not, however, the action for which Fremantle is best remembered. Five years later, in 1829, as commander of the frigate HMS *Challenger*, he landed in Western Australia and hoisted the British flag at Swan River for the first time. The city of Fremantle is named after him.

Nevertheless Charles Fremantle is the anchor for a proud tradition that lives on in the RNLI today. Gold medals, like the Victoria Cross, are awarded only rarely, which underlines the extreme heroism that they signify. Silver and bronze medals are more commonly given but still exemplify extraordinary courage. Sir William Hillary, credited with founding the Institution, won three gold medals on lifeboat rescues. He claimed that one of his proudest moments was when his son Augustus was awarded a silver.

It is not just volunteers for the RNLI who are recognised. Gallantry medals are given to anyone shown to have played

Opposite: The christening of the *Atherfield* lifeboat in the Isle of Wight, 1891.

a significant part in a rescue at sea. Recipients have included lighthouse keepers and their families, coastguards, fishermen, coastal workers who have commandeered boats to effect a rescue, and even schoolboys.

The youngest recipient, Frederick Carter, was 11 when he and his friend, 16-year-old Frank Perry, rowed their small boat into rough water in Weymouth Bay to pick up two men whose craft had capsized owing to the difficult conditions. Carter and Perry were awarded silver medals in June 1890.

With RNLI services now so widespread and efficient, the majority of modern medals have gone to lifeboat crew. At the moment the tally of medals awarded stands at 150 gold, 1,564 silver and 795 bronze.

Today the medals – which bear the image of RNLI founder Sir

Below: *Duke of Northumberland*, the first steam lifeboat.

William Hillary – provide us with a window on the past, a reminder of previous generations who faced down the elements to save lives. While the pluck needed to serve in a lifeboat remains the same, the countenance of the lifeboat service in many areas has changed. Many former lifeboat stations no longer exist. As with the ghost stations on the London Underground, there's little more than stories and shadows to remind people of the vital service that once existed there.

The south-west coast of the Isle of Wight is an excellent example of this. Within the space of five years the crews of lifeboats based at Brighstone Grange, Atherfield and Brooke were involved in two high-profile rescues that loom large in RNLI annals. Yet ultimately all three stations were closed in the wake of better or more appropriate facilities opening nearby.

On 9 March 1888, the *Sirenia* of Glasgow was on its way from San Francisco to Dunkirk with a cargo of wheat when it became stranded on Atherfield Ledge in thick fog. Untypically for foggy weather there was also a heavy sea and the *Sirenia* risked being smashed into the nearby cliffs.

Brighstone Grange's lifeboat *Worcester Cadet* went to her aid, although it took two hours of hard rowing to reach the casualty. On the first trip the lifeboat brought back to shore the master's wife, her three children, a maidservant and a ship's apprentice. The plan was then to return to the vessel at low water, timed for one in the morning, for a safe transfer of the rest of the crew.

Despite the darkness, the *Worcester Cadet* took 13 men aboard for the loss of ten oars to the crushing seas. But the rescue went horribly wrong when the lifeboat was swallowed by a series of mighty waves as they raced to shore. Later, a crew member told the local newspaper the first was 'a huge wave, higher than any of the others, a mountain of black water with a fringe of white at the top'. Against the odds, the lifeboat emerged from the deluge, but was then capsized by a second giant wave. As per design it quickly righted itself, but its coxswain Moses Munt, assistant coxswain Thomas Cotton and two of the *Sirenia*'s crew were drowned.

The lifeboat returned to shore with its remaining crew and passengers, powered more by the sea than by the four remaining oars. The crowd that had gathered on the shore pulled them up the beach.

Overleaf: Lymington B class Atlantic 75 *Victor 'Danny' Lovelock* inshore lifeboat on hand to help the yachts during the Isle of Wight's Round the Island Race.

By noon, when the lifeboat was ready to set off again, three of the men who had been on the ill-fated expedition in the early hours were aboard for their third trip to the ship, despite the effects of hypothermia and exhaustion. This time the remaining 13 men were rescued without incident.

However, the full scale of the tragedy did not unfold until later. The Brooke lifeboat *William Slaney Lewis* had launched and fought its way out towards the *Sirenia*. Unable to safely approach the stricken ship in the swell, it stood by for more than 15 hours, and at one point another violent wave washed three of its crew overboard. Although two were saved thanks to their lifelines attached to the boat, the other, second coxswain Reuben Cooper, drowned in the dark seas. For years the day was referred to as 'Black Saturday'. Later, the Chief Inspector of Lifeboats wrote in his report: 'The perseverance of the men both in the boats and on shore was worthy of admiration.'

It was the *Sirenia* disaster that made a lifeboat station at Atherfield seem both logical and necessary, despite some geographical disadvantages. In February 1891 the Institution's *Journal* recounted the story of its opening:

> It having been considered that a lifeboat placed at Atherfield, on the south-west shore of the Isle of Wight, would be the means of affording material assistance to vessels which are not un-frequently driven on to the ledges of rocks off that dangerous part of the coast, the Royal National Lifeboat Institution decided last year to form a lifeboat station there. Accordingly a corrugated iron boathouse has been erected on the top of the cliff – here about 76 feet high – to the face of which a series of flat skids or sleepers have been securely fastened; over these the lifeboat is lowered by ropes, the incline being 1 in 3 and the distance to the beach about 240 feet. When returning to the boathouse the lifeboat is hauled up by means of a powerful winch. The new boat, which was placed on its station in October last, is 31 feet long, 7¼ feet wide, and rows 10 oars, double-banked. It possesses all the latest improvements, with all the other characteristics of the boats of the Institution in the way of self-righting, self-ejecting water etc. The cost of the new boat and equipment has

been defrayed from a legacy bequeathed to the Institution for the purpose by the late Mrs Swift of Kensington and Chale, the boat being named after her, the *Catherine Swift*.

The London, Brighton and South Coast Railway Company kindly gave the lifeboat a free conveyance over their line from London to Portsmouth, whence it was sailed to its station on 29 October by the crew, who came over specially to fetch it. When off St Catherine's, they found a very heavy hollow sea in the 'race' there; and the Coxswain and crew afterwards reported that the boat behaved admirably and gave them every satisfaction.

There were, unbelievably, seven brothers of the Cotton family in the new crew. Two of them, David and William, won silver medals for their part in the rescue of the *Sirenia* crew as members of the Brighstone Grange lifeboat crew.

Just a year later the *Catherine Swift* was thrust into the thick of a major rescue alongside the *Worcester Cadet* from Brighstone Grange and the *William Slaney Lewis* from the station at Brooke. All responded to the distress rockets fired by the four-masted SS *Eider* of Bremen. Once again the area was fog-bound and the waves were pounding. After a short period of indecision the ship's master decided to land the passengers, so the lifeboats made 18 trips between the vessel and the shore to land 233 people. The next day the rescue continued with a further 146 people brought ashore in 11 trips. Afterwards the lifeboats helped in bringing cargo, including gold and silver bars, mail and luggage from the stricken liner to the safety of the Isle of Wight.

As the Eider's structure was sound, the master and some crew men stayed on board. Several weeks later the ship was towed off the rocks and taken to Southampton docks for repairs.

John Hayter, coxswain of the Brooke lifeboat, and William Cotton, by now Atherfield lifeboat coxswain, won silver medals for their role in both the *Sirenia* and *Eider* rescues. Brighstone lifeboat coxswain James Cotton also won his first silver medal from the RNLI. All three were also given watches by the Emperor of Germany. The inscription on one read: 'We, William, by the grace of God, Emperor of Germany and King of Prussia, grant to the Coxswain of the lifeboat *Worcester Cadet* of Brighstone, Mr James Cotton, this acknowledgement of help rendered to the crew and passengers of the stranded Mail Steamship *Eider* of Bremen when in distress at sea.' The Kaiser also donated £200 to the RNLI.

It was the same 'Kaiser Bill' who led Germany to war against Great Britain 22 years later. And a year after the beginning of the First World War the lifeboat stations at Brighstone Grange and Atherfield were closed. At Brighstone the problem lay with continuing erosion by the sea. At Atherfield the difficulties of launching the lifeboat on such a steep gradient finally spelled its demise. Clearly, initial reports in 1891 which claimed 'the slipway was found to work perfectly while not the least difficulty was experienced in hauling the boat up the steep incline' were overly optimistic. The station at Brooke remained open until 1937.

Another southern lifeboat station was closed after sustaining one of the worst losses of life in RNLI history. On 15 November 1928, two ships collided in the Channel off the Kentish coast, leaving the brick-laden *Alice* severely damaged.

The maroon went up in Rye in the darkness before dawn. As it was low tide it took some time to manoeuvre the lifeboat *Mary Stanford* to the water, and she didn't leave the shore until 6.45 a.m. Just five minutes later a message giving the all-clear came through to Rye coastguard. The crew of the *Alice* had been picked up by another ship. No one was in danger during that grey daybreak – except the lifeboat men themselves.

Three times a maroon was fired to recall the lifeboat, but presumably the signal went unseen, as the boat continued to head out to sea under the power of its oars and sail. At about 10.30 a.m a young boy collecting driftwood watched helplessly as the lifeboat tipped over in a heavy sea outside Rye harbour, the drama illuminated by a single shaft of sunlight. His father duly reported to the lifeguard and soon everyone in Rye clustered on the shore. The final straw of hope was snapped by midday as the upturned lifeboat floated lifelessly to the beach.

The impact on the village could hardly have been greater. Rye's fishing community was all but wiped out by the tragedy as whole families were devastated. The 17 men who died were coxswain Herbert Head and his two sons James and John, second coxswain Joseph Stonham, bowman Henry Cutting with his brothers Robert and Albert, brothers Charles, Robert and Alexander Pope, brothers William and Leslie Clark, cousins Maurice and Arthur Downey, Herbert Smith, Walter Igglesden and Charlie Southerden.

No one knows why the lifeboat overturned, although a light, non-self-righting model had been chosen for the station back in 1914 as it was thought best suited to the lie of the land in Rye. Pictures of it on the beach, lashed by surf, made front-page news. An inquest into the men's deaths looked closely at the condition of the boat and the efficacy of the kapok life jackets worn by the crew, which were potentially waterlogged by the time the men were catapulted into the sea. The inquest recorded verdicts of accidental death. Afterwards the RNLI requested an inquiry by the Board of Trade to scrutinise the safety measures in place at the time.

The inquiry's findings led to the following conclusion: 'As there were no survivors of the crew, the cause of the Lifeboat capsizing is a matter of conjecture, but from the evidence available we are of the opinion that whilst attempting to make the Harbour on a strong flood tide and in high and dangerous breaking sea, she was suddenly capsized and the crew were thrown into the water, two men being entangled under the boat. The broken water and heavy surf caused the loss of the crew.'

Fifteen of the bodies were buried in a communal grave in Rye. A sixteenth, that of Henry Cutting, was added was after being washed up three months later at Eastbourne. However, the body of John Head

THE IMPACT ON THE VILLAGE COULD HARDLY HAVE BEEN GREATER. RYE'S FISHING COMMUNITY WAS ALL BUT WIPED OUT BY THE TRAGEDY

was never recovered. The boat, built in 1916, was taken to London to be dismantled. A commemorative stained-glass window in a local church bears a tribute that ends with the words: 'They went boldly into the last of all their storms.'

The tragedy was compounded by the delay in dispatching the message that no help was needed. Speedier action might have prevented the lifeboat from launching that morning. A year later radio telephones were introduced by the RNLI, which enabled lifeboats to be called home immediately.

One of the busiest stretches of water around the English coast lies off the fortified town of Dover, and for two periods during the 20th century the lifeboat station there was shut. The initial closure coincided with the First World War. When it was reopened in 1919 it was with the *James Stevens No. 3*, the first lifeboat to be powered by screw propeller. It was launched only five times before the station was closed again in 1922.

In the subsequent years, however, there were an increasing number of aeroplanes flying over the English Channel. With flight technology still relatively new, the RNLI was conscious of the likelihood of a plane crash at sea and the need for a lifeboat to attend to an emergency of this nature. As a result the *Sir William Hillary* arrived at Dover in 1930, a new-style, nimble boat powered by two 375-horsepower petrol engines and capable of more than 17 knots. Indeed, it motored at almost twice the speed of most motor lifeboats of the era. Within a decade it was facing a series of challenges that its designers had not contemplated, and a rescue carried out in 1939, two months after the outbreak of the Second World War, highlighted the dilemmas now facing lifeboat crews.

The drama started when the trawler *Blackburn Rovers*, which had been commandeered by the Royal Navy for anti-submarine patrol, ran into difficulties off Dover in a stiff south-westerly. For once, though, it wasn't the worsening conditions and the effects they would wreak on the disabled vessel that occupied the minds of the 16 men aboard. They were in close proximity to minefields laid throughout the Channel to scupper German invasion plans. After the anchor failed to hold the ship to the sea floor it seemed more likely that *Blackburn Rovers* would be scuppered.

The Dover lifeboat was launched with Lieutenant Richard Walker of the Royal Naval Reserve aboard, clutching charts that revealed the whereabouts of minefields in the Channel. Although the *Sir William Hillary* was fast, conditions at sea were poor and it took more than an hour to reach the trawler. And, in accordance with wartime procedure, the first priority was to offload all sensitive papers from the Navy vessel, to prevent them falling into enemy hands.

By now the trawler was rolling uncontrollably, making it almost impossible to come alongside. Worse, the two vessels had drifted into

Above: The RNLI are alerted that three men have mysteriously jumped from a Stena Line ferry. With the help of an RAF chopper two men are spotted and picked up – but they throw something suspicious in the water, which the RNLI recover.

a minefield. If either brushed one of the explosive devices that dotted the water, both would be blown to pieces. When the paperwork and portable equipment had finally been removed, the crew made a perilous transfer to the lifeboat and the trawler had to be sunk.

For more than an hour the hearts of lifeboat men and sailors raced, before they finally turned and headed for home. With waves regularly breaking over the lifeboat, it took three hours to reach the safety of the harbour. Coxswain Colin Bryant, still recovering from a recent illness, was given a silver medal for his tenacity, and four other men aboard the *Sir William Hillary* that day received bronze medals.

Minefields, enemy aircraft, U-boats and prowling E-boats became an everyday reality for men manning the lifeboats during the Second World War. An abundance of bravery was shown on every call-out. During the Dunkirk evacuation, when many men of the British Expeditionary Force were rescued under fire by an assortment of small craft, the lifeboats and some of their crews went willingly into the terror.

In the early afternoon of 30 May 1940, the Ministry of Shipping called on the RNLI to send as many lifeboats as possible to Dover, at speed. No further information was given and nothing was asked. Thousands of men in the British Expeditionary Force (BEF) were being overrun by the Germans' lightning advance through France. Pressed from all sides, the soldiers had only one option, to head for the sandy beaches of Dunkirk. From there it was the job of the Royal Navy to bring as many back home as possible in order that Britain could fight another day.

Operation Dynamo had already swung into action before the call for help went out to the RNLI. But, as the crisis there became acute, more boats were needed. Nineteen lifeboats and their crews responded to the call, from Shoreham Harbour in the west to Gorleston in Norfolk, 110 miles to the north of Dover up the east coast.

A problem arose almost instantly between the Royal Navy officers organising this mammoth rescue and the lifeboat crews. The navy men believed the lifeboats could be taken into the beaches to ferry men to destroyers and other large vessels waiting offshore. The lifeboat men knew, from their years of experience, and now insisted, that their motorised craft were no good for this purpose and that small, oared boats would be needed. (For lifeboat men it seemed symptomatic of an attitude among servicemen, who used to keep them at arm's length in all offshore rescues – when it was their lifeboats, they felt, that were best placed to rescue men from downed aircraft and torpedoed ships.)

As a result only two lifeboats – from Ramsgate and Margate – crossed the Channel with their own crews at the controls. The rest were requisitioned by irate navy commanders and had navy men at the helm. Equally incensed, many lifeboat men went home to sail their own fishing boats to the French coast as part of a flotilla of small, privately owned ships. To counter the problems on the beaches foreseen by fellow lifeboat men, Ramsgate lifeboat

Opposite: Lifeboat men attempt to ferry soldiers to safety at Dunkirk in 1940.

Left: Norfolk and Suffolk class lifeboat *Agnes Cross*.

coxswain Howard Primrose Knight put to sea towing eight small rowing boats behind.

His lifeboat, *Prudential*, left at 2.20 p.m. with a crew of eight, who swapped their usual sailor or flat caps for steel helmets, and with a cargo of drinking water for soldiers on the beaches. On their way across the Channel they sailed past assorted vessels heading for Britain, loaded with evacuated soldiers.

As they came close to Dunkirk the full horror began to unfold. The air was thick with fumes from two burning oil tanks in the town, while the sand dunes behind several miles of beach were black with columns of men, exhausted and desperate. Sea channels were clogged with the wreckage of boats that had already been destroyed by enemy fire. And waves of Luftwaffe bombers continued to fill the sky, a dull throb becoming an ear-splitting roar on their approach. In response to their appearance there were blasts of anti-aircraft fire. The sea, covered with oil, was also littered with magnetic mines recently dropped by German aircraft.

Prudential arrived at Dunkirk at 8 p.m. and turned east, heading for a section of beach called Malo. Under cover of darkness the coxswain dispatched to the beach three small boats which returned full of men. A dozen naval men manned another three small boats to extend the operation, but they failed to return to *Prudential*. However, before the night was out, four small boats were ferrying between beach and boat until it was packed with 160 men. Then the lifeboat headed further out to sea to offload bedraggled, shocked soldiers, armed but often half-naked, on to a ship standing by in deeper waters.

This continued until 800 men were on the larger ship, which was then ready to return to England. It was strength-sapping work for the lifeboat men, who had to hold their boats steady in the surf while soldiers got aboard in addition to pulling oars.

By dawn, Coxswain Knight went inshore to look for three missing rowing boats. He found only one of them, empty and abandoned on the beach, among a litter of wreckage.

Daylight brought a new wave of bombing, and the navigation for rowing boats was becoming increasingly challenging, with surf being whipped up by the edge of an Atlantic storm. Still the lifeboat crew fetched as many soldiers as it could from shore to ship. With the possibilities of escape narrowing on Malo beach, the lifeboat headed for La Panne at the request of an outlying destroyer.

By the following day the lifeboat had helped bring 2,800 men to the larger boats that would take them to England. With her crew exhausted and her small boats wrecked or missing, it was time to turn for home too. By the time they got back to Dover the men had been working for 40 hours, mostly under fire.

Margate lifeboat *Lord Southborough*, commanded by coxswain Edward Parker, left England under tow, but when they arrived at Nieuport, east of Dunkirk, at midnight the barge towing it ran

Below: Margate lifeboat *Lord Southborough* took load after load of soldiers from Dunkirk under continuous shelling, bombing and aerial machine-gun fire.

aground and proved impossible to shift. In darkness the lifeboat made tentative progress towards the shore. Immediately they were detailed to bring the patients from La Panne hospital to safety. Then it was the turn of a group of French servicemen.

Without rowing boats to bring men off the beach, it was down to the lifeboat men to haul troops queuing in shoulder-high water into the high-sided craft. Fortunately Coxswain Parker had taken ten crew men rather than the usual eight. The first boatload of 80 Frenchmen were taken back to the barge – still stranded on a sandbar – and the lifeboat returned for a collection of men from the Border Regiment. The increased weight of the lifeboat now pushed the keel hard into the sand. Nervously, the men waited in darkness punctuated by bombs, bullets and the cries of the injured, for the tide to change.

Back went the lifeboat, as soldiers still poured down the sand dunes on to the beaches in orderly files, desperate for rescue. Most men held their rifles aloft as they plunged into the chilly water to reach the lifeboat. One man held his banjo alongside his rifle. When the coxswain urged him to drop them for his own safety, the man discarded the weapon but clung to the banjo, and he was soon strumming quietly in his seat as he waited for the boat to be filled.

A decade later Coxswain Parker recorded his memories of the Dunkirk trip, which began when he summoned his crew who were standing by in their favourite pub.

> Margate was a pretty dead town then with more than half the population evacuated, but it was a different story when we got to Dunkirk. With shells bursting and fires raging, it was like hell.
>
> Our first job all through that night was to take the wounded from La Panne hospital, which was being shelled, and transfer them to a destroyer. Some were floated out to us

Above: Littlehampton's volunteer lifeboat crew save a dog in distress in their D class inshore lifeboat. The coastguard requested they launch after reports that Buster, a Jack Russell terrier, had entered the harbour. When they reached Buster he was actually underwater before they pulled him out cold and shaking – but alive!

on rafts and others carried out by soldiers who waded through water holding them over their heads.

    On Friday we were ferrying men off to different ships when I heard a squeaking in the boat and thought it was our engine, hoping nothing was going to happen to our engine over there. We searched all around and we found it was a French soldier with a guinea pig under his tunic and this was making the noise.

Overleaf: The wreck of the *South Goodwin* lightship on Goodwin Sands. She broke from her anchors in winds of over 80 mph and only one man survived.

Later, the commander of the destroyer HMS *Icarus*, which made six trips between Dover and Dunkirk during Operation Dynamo, wrote: 'The magnificent behaviour of the crew of the Margate lifeboat who, with no thought of rest, brought off load after load of soldiers from Dunkirk under continuous shelling, bombing and aerial machine-gun fire, will be an inspiration to us as long as we live.'

    When the morning brought an increase in the size of the surf, the lifeboat could no longer broach the shore but remained out of white water, pulling to safety men afloat on smaller boats or buoyant wreckage. At one point, the crew looked about them to see that theirs was the only boat not smashed or submerged. Floating in the water were bodies of men who had failed to board rescue boats and had not the strength to get back to the sand. The last batch of men rescued by the Margate lifeboat were 17 remaining Royal Navy sailors who had been among 150 sent to supervise the mass departure from the beach.

    Together they made for Dover on 31 May, as Operation Dynamo began to wind up. The *Lord Southborough* had been out of port for more than 24 hours and brought 600 men off the beaches. When the evacuation ended, as German forces finally took control of Dunkirk, a total of 338,226 men had been rescued.

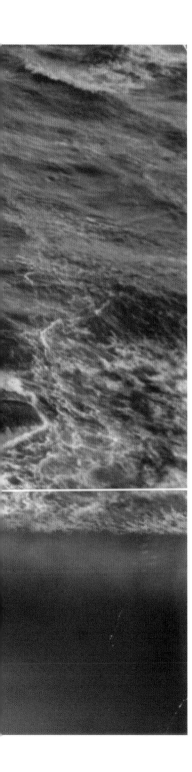

More than 68,000 were killed, wounded or captured while a total of 243 ships were sunk, including six Royal Navy destroyers.

The south coast is home to one of the RNLI's important campaigners. Sonny Wells, former soldier, soccer player and golfer, was drawn to the beachside playground at Southsea, Portsmouth, on a hot day in May 2009 when he was 20 years old. He dived from the pier, a feat he'd performed on previous occasions. But this time he misjudged the depth of the seawater and the lie of the land beneath – and broke his neck.

Jumping or diving from cliffs, piers and the like into tidal waters is called tombstoning, and it has become increasingly popular. Between 2006 and 2010 RNLI boats were called to 73 tombstoning accidents, rescued 39 people and saved six lives.

Wells acknowledges: 'Everyone thinks they are invincible. I did myself.' Since being paralysed from the chest down his life has changed beyond recognition. 'I was very active – I'd been in the army, was a keen footballer, I was always on my toes – until I dived off the pier in Southsea. It was something I'd done before, but this time I broke my neck in three places and now suffer the consequences of being in a wheelchair for the rest of my life.

'Three-quarters of my body doesn't work, so from being an able-bodied person to how I am now is a massive change. It's not just changed my life, it's changed my family's life. Just for that five minutes of madness, it's not worth it.'

His mother Jacqui Unal gave permission for pictures of her son in a coma to be used to warn others about the perils of tombstoning. Sonny has since become a vocal campaigner against the activity, which is popular with young men.

Young people like Sonny are important to the RNLI. Across the Solent Max Rimington is another valued member of the team, although he is barely out of school. Growing up in Malaysia ensured that Max learned two valuable lessons about his relationship with the sea. The first was that he loved sailing with a passion, handling a yacht from the tender age of six under supervision from his parents. Just as importantly, he understood what happened when things went wrong; especially when no lifeboat was around to race to the rescue.

'I heard some real horror stories out there,' recalls Max, now 18 and a volunteer at Cowes RNLI station, Isle of Wight. 'In Malaysia they have nothing equivalent to the RNLI, and so if you get into trouble you're very much on your own. I remember incidents in which people made it on to life rafts but were never located. Others where crews lost their lives on a sinking boat simply because there was no lifeboat to call.

'When our family returned to the UK, those memories made me determined to join the RNLI. It really is such a precious service to anyone out on the water.'

Max, a former pupil of Medina High School in Newport, Isle of Wight, joined the Cowes crew as a shore-based volunteer at 16 – the youngest age for a new recruit. Although he was then too young to assist at rescues, he regards the time as a valuable apprenticeship, learning the basics of RNLI service along with the handling and maintenance skills that keep the station's Atlantic 85 inshore boat *Tabby Cat* operational.

'You do all the grass-roots stuff such as fundraising and social events,' says Max. 'Like most volunteers I've certainly got hot and sweaty shaking a bucket in the High Street. To me, the crew nights were a fantastic introduction. You're made very welcome, you have a bit of a laugh together and you get to feel part of the team. When you're on a shout there's only three or four of you in the boat. You need to trust every one of them and know that they're there for you.'

Britain's south coast is busy enough with sea traffic funnelling through the English Channel. But the region also includes four lifeboat stations on the tidal Thames: at Gravesend, Tower, Chiswick and Teddington. There are 10 full-time staff who crew the boats at Gravesend, Tower and Chiswick and about 40 volunteers.

A shortfall in life-saving cover on the Thames was identified after 51 people died in 1989, in the wake of a collision between the *Marchioness* pleasure cruiser and the dredger *Bowbelle*. For the first time, following a request by the government made via the coastguard service, the RNLI would provide its search and rescue services on a river rather than estuary waters or the open sea.

The Tower station opened for the first time on 2 January 2002. Since then it has become the most called-on station in the country, and in 2010 had its busiest year yet when it responded to 491 emergencies.

Opposite: Tower E class lifeboat on the Thames, with the Houses of Parliament behind.

Overleaf: Tower E class lifeboat with the London Eye in the background.

According to statistics, the station is responsible for 208 lives being saved since its opening, 25 of which were saved in 2010. That figure reflects only the number of people who would not be alive today without the presence of a lifeboat on the London station. As the RNLI often works in conjunction with the police, fire and harbour authority boats, it is safe to assume that the lifeboat men from Tower have been an integral part of life-saving operations on many more occasions.

In the heart of London's tourist attractions, the station is open around the clock and responds within 90 seconds to an emergency call. Any casualty between Teddington and Canvey Island can expect to see an RNLI boat motoring to their aid within 15 minutes of making a call. Kevin Maynard, who is helmsman of the lifeboat at Tower, joined the RNLI in 2001, aged 23, just prior to the opening of the station.

'I'd always been interested in the RNLI, but it was quite difficult to get involved with lifeboats when I was growing up in Chessington, Surrey, which was nowhere near the sea,' he explains.

Seaside holidays in childhood made him aware of the service and, like generations of children, he lapped up information about the RNLI through the children's television programme *Blue Peter,* which had regular lifeboat appeals. In its long history *Blue Peter* has asked viewers to donate items including jewellery, paperback books and tin foil and it has raised sufficient funds to buy 28 lifeboats.

For Maynard the most memorable operation he took part in occurred soon after he joined the service. 'A couple who lived on a houseboat just below Tower Bridge were expecting a baby and decided to have a home birth. But when the midwives looked at the gangway on to the houseboat they decided it wasn't safe enough for themselves and all their equipment.

'When the woman went into labour we took a midwife to the boat and helped her on through a porthole. And when she had to leave at the end of her shift we took another midwife to the houseboat and picked up the first one. The second midwife delivered the baby, who was healthy. We collected her from the houseboat afterwards. Later we delivered some presents to the new parents for the baby.'

Usually, the call-outs are less happy occasions. There are a number of people who threaten suicide from London's bridges and riverfront buildings. Then there are people who fall into the river by accident.

'Recently we were called out after a teenage girl went into the water. She was leaning over the railings of Hungerford footbridge taking a photo, wearing a backpack full of books. She leant over so far that she fell in.'

Then there are a number of people who believe the River Thames is a safe place for a swim. 'It isn't something we would recommend,' says Maynard, who warned that it was full of currents, eddies and undertows that are treacherous in the extreme. It is also a busy waterway, with large numbers of both freight and leisure

craft. Many of the calls that come to the Tower station concern broken-down boats. And there are many people who fall ill on or by the Thames that need attention. 'We can get there before an ambulance, check how seriously hurt the patient is and provide first aid.'

Even before he joined the RNLI, Maynard had an extensive knowledge of the Thames. Previously he drove passenger boats up and down the river, after a five-year apprenticeship to gain his Watermen and Lightermen's licence, which made him a river-going equivalent of the London cabbie, with similar proven local knowledge.

During 7/7 – the terrorist attacks in London that killed 52 people in 2005 – the Thames lifeboats as well as one from Sheerness were put on stand-by and went to Canary Wharf to help ferry office workers out of the city after large parts of the public transport system closed down. No one knew if there were more atrocities in the offing. 'We wanted to be proactive rather than reactive,' Maynard says.

Along with other crew, Maynard works 12-hour night and day shifts to ensure the station has round-the-clock cover, dressed in a dry suit that's turned down at the waist. The coastguard calls come through on a specially designated telephone that rings inside and out of the station. He is then on the water in a matter of seconds. Having pulled up his dry suit and grabbed a life jacket and helmet, he is only a few steps away from the lifeboat moored on the river next to the station pontoon.

Maynard and his crew use an 'E' class lifeboat which is ideal for use in river shallows and has plenty of deck space. In use since 2002, it operates with a crew of three and can travel at a maximum of 40 knots thanks to its water-jet engines. Equipment aboard includes radar, radio, blue lights, a siren and night-vision equipment. There are six in the RNLI fleet. In an emergency the E class lifeboat can accommodate 20 people and it will tow an inflatable rescue craft that can carry 60 more.

SOUTH-WEST

PORTLAND
PLYMOUTH
SOLE
LUNDY

Prevailing winds have taken every opportunity to drive passing ships into the granite embrace of Britain's south-west coast. Fringed with diamond-sharp rocks that can slice into the keel of even the sturdiest ship, it is a coast where the best and the worst of British weather is reflected. Coves which seem sandy and benign on a summer's day are soon turned into tumbling whirlpools in a gale, sluicing men and ships to their doom. Cliffs that capture a thousand soft shades at sunset loom grey and foreboding in storms, when they are capable of reducing ships' timber to matchwood.

Nowhere has the tenacity of lifeboat men with their 'try, try and try again' philosophy been put to the test more often, or the fine line between tragedy and triumph been more frequently and painfully illustrated.

In Penzance during Queen Victoria's reign the lifeboat *Richard Lewis* was often called upon when poor weather swept up the foot of England. On 6 December 1868, it was summoned to Mount's Bay when the barque *North Britain* of Southampton went aground in high seas and raging winds.

Six of the ship's crew were drowned when the boat they released in a bid to reach shore was swamped and turned turtle. Four others survived after being pushed to land by the surf and then pulled to safety by the waiting crowd.

The lifeboat nonetheless prepared to launch, as there were crew men who remained at grave risk on the ship. Fighting a course through Atlantic peaks and troughs, the lifeboat came alongside for a matter of moments before being upturned. It was a self-righting lifeboat built to James Peake's design, which was derived from all the best bits taken from the entrants into the 1851 competition. Fortunately none of the crew died, but several were injured, including the coxswain, Thomas Carbis, so the lifeboat turned back and made the mile and a half return journey, to find plenty of people waiting to help boat and men out of the water. But when a call went out for a new crew to replace the exhausted and drenched men recently returned, for a moment there was hesitation. Then a voice was heard.

'I'll try again,' volunteered William Higgans, one of the initial crew who'd recovered quickly. Soon others followed his lead. This time William Blackmore of the Penzance coastguard was nominated

COVES WHICH SEEM SANDY AND BENIGN ON A SUMMER'S DAY ARE SOON TURNED INTO TUMBLING WHIRLPOOLS IN A GALE, SLUICING MEN AND SHIPS TO THEIR DOOM

coxswain, and the French vice-consul took one of the oars. The eight remaining crew on the barque were pulled to safety moments before the grounded vessel disintegrated.

That same month the doggedness of lifeboat men in the south-west was put to the test again on the North Devon coast. This time it was a north-westerly wind whipping up white water to the horizon. The Appledore lifeboat *Hope*, named after the Hope family who donated cash for its purchase, was called into action when an Austrian barque, the *Pace*, ran into difficulties in Bideford Bay. The lifeboat was moved into position, hauled on its carriage by five pairs of horses. A dozen men began pulling oars and before too long it drew into the lee of the stricken *Pace*, close enough to throw a rope towards its masts.

Below: Padstow Tamar class lifeboat *Spirit of Padstow* launches down the slipway.

Left: Torbay Severn class lifeboat *Alec and Christina Dykes* keeping ahead of the spray.

However, there were no bodies clinging to the rigging – usually perceived to be the safest place when a ship ran into trouble. Nor were there any faces peering over the deck rail. It was eerily quiet. Suddenly a boy launched himself from the ship to the lifeboat, almost into the arms of the bowman. His frantic signs led lifeboat men to believe there were more people on board. And, sure enough, after a few moments eight men came tumbling into the *Hope*. But what seemed like a successful rescue came close to disaster when a wave smashed the lifeboat into the body of the *Pace*. Not only was the lifeboat stern snapped off, coxswain Joseph Cox was caught and almost crushed between the two vessels. Cox – who was coxswain at Appledore for 21 years before his retirement in 1873 – was winded, but his cork life jacket saved him from serious injury.

Using an oar in place of a rudder, the lifeboat made for the safety of the bay, conscious that men remained aboard the *Pace*. Once the survivors were back on dry land a new crew was recruited for a second mission. Three men from the first, including Cox, were among them.

This time a roaring wave was enough to tip over the lifeboat before it even reached the *Pace*, where survivors were now aloft in the rigging after abandoning their captain's early plan to stay and salvage the ship. Fortunately, the *Hope* was a self-righting boat, but all the crew were left floundering in freezing seas before, one by one, they hauled themselves or were pulled by others into the boat. Cox, still bruised from his previous encounter with the *Pace*, came off worst again, being in the water longer than anyone else. His son, also called Joseph Cox, stepped into his place as coxswain and decided to head for home.

With the tide now falling, men knew they would soon be able to wade to the stranded ship. When they did so, they helped the captain and two of his men to safety. Two others had fallen to their deaths. In recognition of their courage the Emperor of Austria awarded Cox senior and junior and crew member John Kelly the silver cross of merit. They also received silver RNLI medals.

The *Pace* was not the only ship in trouble on the North Devon coast that day. The *Leopard* of London had been blown ashore at nearby Westward Ho! Lifeboat men were unable to fix a line to the ship by using a rocket, so coastguard boatman David Johns – one of the crew on the first expedition to the *Pace* – attached a rope to his waist and

WHAT SEEMED LIKE A SUCCESSFUL RESCUE CAME CLOSE TO DISASTER WHEN A WAVE SMASHED THE LIFEBOAT INTO THE BODY OF THE *PACE*

swam to the vessel. Despite reaching its side he was knocked unconscious by a piece of wreckage before he could climb aboard – and drowned.

Another Appledore man stepped up for the task. This time George Galsworthy succeeded in securing a line and the crew of the *Leopard* were saved.

Further evidence of the lengths to which lifeboat men here will go for ships in distress, is provided by the story of the extraordinary expedition undertaken by the men of Lynmouth in 1899 when they heard about a drama unfolding in a neighbouring bay.

On 12 January 1899, the maroon to summon crew and helpers could only just be heard above the howling gale and driving rain. A telegram had been received at Lynmouth's post office from a hotel keeper at Porlock Weir: 'A vessel is in distress off Gore Point near Porlock. Impossible to launch the Watchet lifeboat because of gale conditions. Can the Lynmouth lifeboat help?'

The ship was the *Forrest Hall*, a three-masted barque weighing some 1,900 tons, which had been under tow up the Bristol Channel

until it collided with its steam tug and damaged it. The tug withdrew to seek repairs, leaving the barque hooked tenuously to the seabed by her anchor. Aboard were 13 crew and five apprentices.

Coxswain Jack Crocombe took one look at the pounding sea and the prevailing wind and knew it would be impossible to launch the lifeboat *Louisa* from Lynmouth. There was only one thing for it: to haul it overland to Porlock, where the wind was more favourable and the casualty would be far closer.

Between Lynmouth and Porlock rises Countisbury Hill, with a gradient of one in four and a half and a height of 1,423 feet. Twenty horses were harnessed to pull the *Louisa* in her launch carriage, a combined weight of about 10 tons, from Lynmouth at sea level. Beyond Countisbury Hill lay Porlock Hill and thereafter an even steeper descent.

At the top of Countisbury Hill a wheel fell off the carriage. In the darkness the men and women accompanying the lifeboat groped on the ground for the missing axle linchpin. With difficulty the wheel was attached and the journey continued.

Now the wide load came to a narrow lane. Undaunted, the villagers manhandled the 34-foot *Louisa* on to skids that had been brought up after the lifeboat by horse and cart. More than 50 years later second coxswain George Richards recalled: 'We could only drag the boat a little way and then stop while the skids behind were picked up, carried forward and laid down in front of her. The road was so narrow that we had a job passing between the boat and the wall.'

Then it was the turn of the horses to haul once more, over open moor. As Devon gave way to Somerset, the *Louisa* was loaded once more on to the launch carriage. It was eight hours before the procession began descending into Porlock, perhaps the most arduous leg of the journey for what was now a band of exhausted men.

At the bottom they began dismantling a garden wall in their path. Hearing the commotion, the wall's owner came out to remonstrate. But when she realised what was happening she pitched in to help pull down the wall. The corner of a shop roof was also removed. Finally, the carriage arrived at the last hurdle, Porlock's pebble beach. In the end the journey had taken ten hours, and there was no time for food or hot drinks as the crew had to find the *Forrest Hall* – and fast.

Opposite: A re-enactment, in authentic costume, of the launch of the Lynmouth lifeboat – including the overground haul with horses to Porlock.

In fact the barque was bearing up well, with her anchors just about holding fast. The *Louisa* stood by until the return of the steam tug, and then her crew helped bring a line between the two. To ensure the safety of the *Forrest Hall*, the *Louisa* accompanied her to South Wales.

The *Louisa* was finally replaced by the *Prichard Frederick Gainer*, in service until Lynmouth's lifeboat station was closed in 1944. As for the *Forrest Hall*, she met her end after running aground off New Zealand's North Island, where her remains can still be seen protruding from the sands on Ninety Mile Beach at low tide.

Some rescues stand out for the sheer volume of lives saved. On 17 March 1907, the lifeboat crews of four Cornish villagers rescued hundreds of people after a White Star liner ran aground off the Lizard when it was cloaked in fog and whipped by a storm. SS *Suevic* was en route from Australia to Liverpool with 382 passengers and 141 crew aboard, and was travelling at full speed at the time of the disaster – caused by a light in a cottage on shore being mistaken for the Lizard lighthouse.

Above: White Star Liner *SS Suevic* against the rocks off the Lizard. Local lifeboat crews rescued 456 people from the wreck.

Overleaf: Coxswain Joseph Cox holding the tiller on the Appledore lifeboat Hope.

Men from the Lizard and Cadgwith lifeboat stations were first on the scene, to find small boats lowered by *Suevic* heading in their direction. Howard Rowley, the RNLI's inspector of lifeboats at the time, takes up the story: 'On the arrival of the Cadgwith and Lizard lifeboats, it was found two of the ship's boats were being sent ashore with women and children and, not being acquainted with the dangerous rocks existing in the vicinity, were in the utmost peril. Had the lifeboats not been at hand they would doubtless never have reached the shore. Such heroic acts deserve to be brought to the notice of all British people.'

The vicar of Cadgwith, the Reverend Harry Vyvyan, was secretary of the lifeboat, something he'd considered to be an honorary post. But that night he went out with the Cadgwith lifeboat *Minnie Moon* and then leapt into one of the liner's boats to guide it into shore. Describing how he commanded the *Suevic* lifeboat through a safe passage he said: 'I went on board to steer her but soon found the six men could hardly pull against the wind. I can tell you I felt jolly proud when she touched the beach and all the women and children were landed safely. Directly I landed my passengers, I stood up in the bows of the boat and called for volunteers to go back with me.'

With some *Suevic* crew Vyvyan attempted to use the same boat to continue the rescue. However, it was smashed against rocks after oarsmen lost control, whereupon he swam back to shore and joined the Lizard lifeboat.

The rescue continued through the night, with lifeboats from Coverack and Porthleven joining the ranks of the rescuers. Meanwhile, women from the Lizard lit fires on the beach and rushed into the water to help children to safety. Of the 160 women and children aboard, 60 were children aged under three.

Between them the lifeboats saved 456 people, including two stowaways. The remainder were brought ashore by tugs after being picked up from the ship's lifeboats. The ship's cargo, which included £400,000 worth of frozen lamb carcasses, was also mostly saved. Afterwards four RNLI men, including the Reverend Vyvyan, and two crew members of *Suevic* all received silver gallantry medals.

THE VICAR OF CADGWITH, THE REVEREND HARRY VYVYAN, WAS SECRETARY OF THE LIFEBOAT, SOMETHING HE'D CONSIDERED TO BE AN HONORARY POST. BUT THAT NIGHT HE WENT OUT WITH THE LIFEBOAT

In its edition of 21 March 1907, the local newspaper *The West Briton* paid a glowing tribute to *Suevic*'s master, Captain Thomas Jones. 'Was there any suggestion of a panic?' its correspondent wrote. 'None whatever. I have never seen better behaviour in my life. One must remember the cigar of Captain Jones. If anything could stop a panic it would be a man who could keep the ash on the end of his cigar in a gale and an emergency.'

The report continued: 'The bravery and self-sacrifice of the women of Cadgwith came in for much commendation. They worked like slaves in turning the winch which drew the lifeboats ashore, and one woman was most heroic, rushing into the sea to her waist and carrying the children ashore. The pluck displayed by the women ... was simply grand.'

The wrecked *Suevic* was left with her bow firmly rammed into the rocks, while her stern was still afloat and intact. Rather than write off the seven-year-old ship, her owners the White Star Line came up with a curious plan. Using dynamite charges, salvagers separated the bow from the stern, which was duly towed to Southampton. Then the Belfast shipbuilders Harland & Wolff constructed another bow, which was attached to the section of the *Suevic*'s stern, giving the ship many more years of service.

But alongside stories of immense humanity, the south-west's history is studded with tales of maritime disasters that left small communities to count the cost.

Nine crew of the St Ives lifeboat were decorated for their part in the rescue of sailors from the 4,000-ton SS *Alba*, driven ashore in bad weather at the end of January 1938. Coxswain Thomas Cocking steered the self-righting motor lifeboat *Caroline Parsons* alongside to bring 23 men off the wreck.

All but three on the lifeboat were then dumped in the water when a wave overturned it. The trio quickly fished everyone they could from the water but then found the boat's engine would not start. Inevitably, the lifeboat was planted on the rocks. Shore helpers rushed to the scene to aid lifeboat crew and seamen, but five sailors from the *Alba* drowned.

But a year later it was five of those award winners who were killed when the self-righting *John and Sarah Eliza Stych* overturned three

times during a storm. The twin events, which still loom large in St Ives, did nothing to deter recently retired coxswain Tommy Cocking from a career with the lifeboat. His great-grandfather was coxswain Thomas Cocking, who died that night in 1939 with great-uncles John Cocking and Richard Stevens. His grandfather, also called Thomas, won a bronze medal for his part in the *Alba* rescue but was not part of the crew that perished. Despite a history weighted with grief, Tommy and his father didn't hesitate when it came to volunteering.

Nor are stories of success and sorrow confined to the pages of distant history. On 13 December 1981 the *Bonita,* of Equador, was in trouble in the middle of the English Channel. Thirty-six people aboard were at risk, as were other users of the busy Channel routes, as she posed a threat to shipping.

Guernsey lifeboat men manned the *Sir William Arnold*, although it didn't take an experienced seafarer's eye to realise conditions were challenging. Southerly winds were blowing with hurricane force, whisking sea spray high into the air to meet squally snow falling from the sky. It made for poor visibility when sightlines were crucial for the sort of rescue that lay ahead.

By the time the lifeboat approached *Bonita* she was listing and helpless. Although it was almost nightfall, wreckage including timber and container drums were still visible cluttering the surface of the water.

Regardless of the hazards, coxswain Michael Scales made no fewer than 50 approaches to the ship, taking 29 people to safety during an operation that lasted three and a half hours. Each occasion called for excellent seamanship skills and intense concentration. To maintain this level of physical and mental focus and keep exhaustion at bay was no mean feat. A further five crew men were saved by helicopter and one by a tug before the *Bonita* sank. One man drowned that night – but the human cost would have been far greater had it not been for Scales and his crew. For his judgement and perseverance Scales won the RNLI gold medal. All of his seven-strong crew received the bronze medal.

Delight in this conquest of the elements was short-lived, however. Less than a week later in the same stretch of ocean, the Penlee lifeboat *Solomon Browne* was lost with all hands in a doomed attempt to rescue those aboard a coaster halted by engine trouble off Land's End in Cornwall.

SOUTHERLY WINDS WERE BLOWING WITH HURRICANE FORCE, WHISKING SEA SPRAY HIGH INTO THE AIR TO MEET SQUALLY SNOW FALLING FROM THE SKY

Union Star, weighing in at 1,400 tons and on its maiden voyage, lost power after seawater seeped into her fuel tanks on 19 December. Captain Henry 'Mick' Moreton was mindful of veering ever closer to the rocky Cornish coast and of the presence on board of his family.

At first it seemed the lifeboat would not be necessary that night. A Sea King helicopter from RAF Culdrose was scrambled to pick up the passengers. A Dutch salvage tug was also heading towards *Union Star*, ready to bring it under tow. But as winds continued to increase, the helicopter found it impossible to engineer a rescue. Even at 400 feet it was being washed down with sea spray. The rest of the story is best told through the clipped radio messages sent and received across the sea – and heard by lifeboat crew's families on scanners in Mousehole.

> **20.47: Penlee Lifeboat to *Union Star*:** Understand you had trouble with the chopper ... do you want for us to come alongside and take the women and children, over.
> ***Union Star* to Penlee Lifeboat:** Yes please. The helicopter is having a bit of difficulty getting to us, so if you could pop out I'll be very much obliged, over.

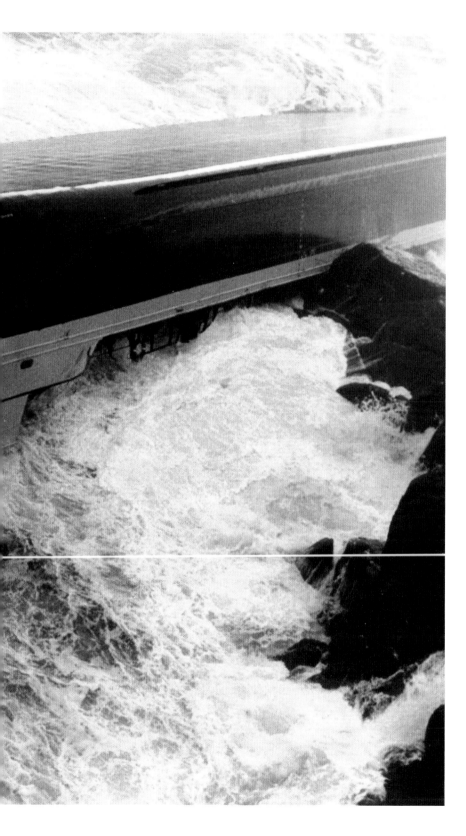

The lifeboat held back while there was another last-ditch effort by the crew of the Sea King to drop a line on board. The *Solomon Browne* approached only after the helicopter crew finally admitted defeat. As *Union Star* had dropped anchor and was swinging with the waves it demanded extraordinary skill to come alongside. Then the anchor chain snapped and the coaster was tossed like flotsam by the 40-foot waves.

>**20.54: Penlee Lifeboat to *Union Star*:** Advise you with crew, everybody to come off, over.
>***Union Star* to Penlee Lifeboat:** Yes, we're all coming off.

For the next half-hour the *Solomon Browne* made continual attempts to get alongside the coaster in winds broaching 100mph. At one point she was carried on top of the coaster and remained there for a few moments before sliding, stern first, back into the waves. All the while, both craft were getting closer to the shore. Finally coxswain Trevelyan Richards spotted a few seconds' respite and slipped alongside.

>**21.21 Penlee Lifeboat to *Falmouth Coastguard*:** This is the Penlee Lifeboat. Penlee Lifeboat calling Falmouth Coastguard.
>***Falmouth Coastguard*:** Penlee Lifeboat. Go.
>**Penlee Lifeboat:** We got four men off – look, er, hang on – we got four off at the moment, er, ma– male and female. There's two left on board …

At that point there was a loud noise and the message ended. Radio contact was lost.

Perhaps bizarrely, that wasn't the moment the *Solomon Browne* was lost. The helicopter crew, returning to base, saw her battling out to sea after broadcasting that last message, presumably to escape the clutches of the rocks. Tug skipper Guy Buurman saw her silhouetted on the crest of a wave and reported at 21.45 that she was 'very close to shore'. It was the last glimpsed sighting of her.

Opposite: The wreckage of the *Solomon Browne*.

Overleaf: The RNLI memorial bearing the names of those who died in the Penlee disaster.

▸ P Morrison · MARGATE ▸ 1857

Mason · A Mille

1891 ▸ S Hart · W Ryan · J Sult

▸ J Pentreath · 1981 ▸ JR Blewe

EB Kinnin · RAMSGATE ▸ 1873

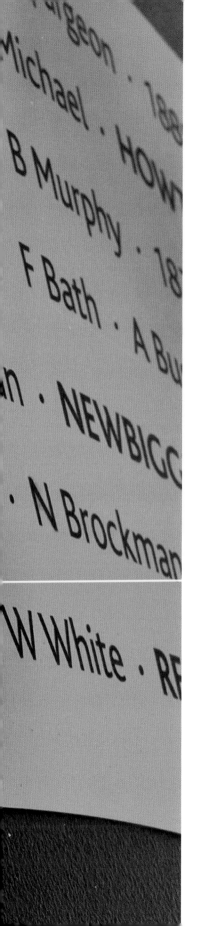

It is now thought that after pulling out to sea Trevelyan Richards and his crew went back for two people on board and two in the water. One theory is that *Union Star* then snagged a reef and flipped over, swamping the lifeboat in the process. Whatever happened, it was with extreme force, as the lifeboat was shattered into small pieces, although almost each one was still recognisable by the distinctive livery of the RNLI. Bit by bit, fragments were washed up ashore. For its part, *Union Star* was found overturned on rocks the next day.

At home people who heard the abrupt end of the conversation hoped for the best but feared the worst. Now it was a one-sided plea for contact, calmly made.

> Penlee Lifeboat, Falmouth Coastguard, over.
> Penlee Lifeboat. Rescue Eight Zero. If you read me fire
> one flare ... if you read me fire a flare.
> Can you hear us, Trev?
> What is your position?
> Do you need any help?
> Shall we come out, Trev?

Hopes that the lifeboat had only suffered a radio problem were dashed when wreckage began to appear, accompanied by the tell-tale waft of diesel.

In a statement submitted to the RNLI by Sea King pilot Lieutenant-Commander Russell L. Smith, an American officer on attachment at Culdrose in 1981, tribute was paid to the heroism of the men aboard the *Solomon Browne*.

'Throughout the entire rescue evolution the Penlee crew never appeared to hesitate,' wrote Smith. 'After each time they were washed, blown or bumped away from the casualty the Penlee lifeboat immediately commenced another run-in. Their spirit and dedication was amazing considering the horrific hurricane seas and the constant pounding they were taking. The greatest act of courage that I have ever seen, and am likely to ever see, was the penultimate courage showed by the Penlee lifeboat when it manoeuvred back alongside the casualty in over 60-foot breakers and rescuing four people [sic] ... they were truly the bravest eight men I've ever seen.'

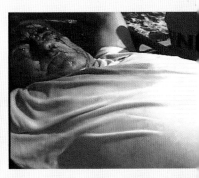

The crew of the *Solomon Browne* who died that night, in addition to those on *Union Star*, on whom there were no survivors, were coxswain Trevelyan Richards, second coxswain James Madron, Nigel Brockman, John Blewett, Charles Greenhaugh, Kevin Smith, Barrie Torrie and Gary Wallis. Posthumously, Trevelyan Richards received the gold medal and the rest bronze for the rescues they carried out before they died.

One young man was turned away from the lifeboat that night. Neil Brockman, whose father Nigel was lifeboat mechanic, was told by Richards: 'No more than one from a family on a night like this.' Neil, who went on to become coxswain of the replacement lifeboat, recalled:

> Quite honestly I wasn't worried about Dad. I was just a kid and it never occurred to me that the boat might be lost. But by 11 p.m. I started thinking: should be job done by now.
>
> Someone told me that radio contact had been lost. That never happens. You're in a gale, you call in every 15 minutes. I got a neighbour to drive me to Newlyn and spoke to the harbourmaster Andrew Munson, who is now our Lifeboat Operations Manager. He said: 'They can't get hold of them, but it could be anything.'
>
> I went home with my mother and brother and waited. As time went on it became obvious what had happened. The Watson class boats were fantastic – they'd go anywhere with enough sea room – but the crew were caught in the worst possible place in conditions the like of which I never want to see again. It was a terrible time for the families.
>
> Despite everything there was no shortage of men coming forward to form a new lifeboat crew. I was back within two days of Dad's death. It's in your blood and you can't escape it.

Above: Speed was of the essence for the Torbay RNLI crew volunteers after a fisherman fell from a quarry platform. The elderly man suffered a significant head injury and was still in the water when the crew of the inshore lifeboat arrived at the scene.

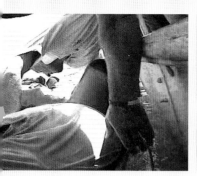

It was a south-west coxswain and crew at the heart of one of the most remarkable rescues of recent years. A catastrophic shift in its cargo of wood left the 6,395-ton vessel *Ice Prince* listing in gale-force winds and rough seas 34 miles off the South Devon coast on 13 January 2008.

The Brixham coastguard called on the lifeboats from Torbay and Salcombe, which worked in concert with the coastguard rescue helicopter. The Royal navy frigate HMS *Cumberland* also joined the rescue, by positioning herself so as to provide shelter. As the ship lost power so the Torbay lifeboat accelerated to its position, at 20 knots clearing much of the water en route.

Initially the lifeboats used powerful searchlights to illuminate the stricken ship as a dozen crew men were winched off by the helicopter. It was a perilous operation, with three winch cables snapping. When the helicopter departed at full capacity it was time for the Torbay lifeboat to approach the *Ice Prince*, by now poised at an impossible angle and dwarfing the lifeboat. The operation was hindered by submerged sections of the ship, and all the while the lifeboat men and crew knew that another lurch in the balance of the freight could send the ship on a final roll from which it would not recover. If that happened the lifeboat would be in terrible danger.

It took more than 50 approaches before the remaining eight crew were safely transferred in an operation that lasted one and three-quarter hours. At one point a crew man who mistimed his jump slithered into the sea just as the lifeboat smacked into the *Ice Prince*. Instantly the Salcombe lifeboat, which had been standing by, roared into action. However, by climbing up some of the vessel that was already underwater, the man made his way back to fellow crew members unassisted.

With the crew now even more reluctant to jump between ship and bobbing lifeboat, it fell to the lifeboat men to lean forward and grab them. Coxswain Mark Criddle was awarded a silver medal for his part in the rescue, while his crew received the 'Thanks of the Institution' inscribed on vellum.

Much later Criddle said: 'We went up to the stern of the ship and took the crew off the port shoulder. They took a leap of faith towards us. Our crew members were reaching out and pulling them in on top of the boat.

'We could quite easily have lost somebody that night. I was more nervous the next day watching it back than I was on the night. I think adrenalin kicks in.'

The medal, he said, was for the station rather than himself. 'The rescue is all about the station, not about any individual. There is a saying that the coxswain can't go without the crew but the crew can go without the coxswain. It is all about training, it is all about being part of something. It is a way of life.'

The *Ice Prince*, rolling in gale-force winds and rough seas, before she disappeared under the waves.

COXSWAIN CRIDDLE SHOWED GREAT LEADERSHIP AND DIRECTION DURING THE RESCUE OPERATION WHEN HE AND HIS CREW SAVED THE LIVES OF EIGHT MEN IN PERILOUS CONDITIONS

RNLI Divisional Inspector Simon Pryce said later: 'Coxswain Criddle showed great leadership and direction during the rescue operation when he and his crew saved the lives of eight men in perilous conditions – conditions that were severe enough to cripple a 6,395-gross-ton ship. The crew were well aware of the dangers they faced, but recognised that the eight crew of the *Ice Prince* were in a life-threatening situation. The actions taken by the Coxswain and lifeboat crew were done under the absolute belief that the *Ice Prince* could capsize and sink at any moment.

'The crew of the lifeboat showed tremendous bravery, tenacity and strength, acting as a well-trained, efficient team. Coxswain Criddle's boat handling skills were put to the test during the rescue – even though he pushed the lifeboat to its limits and made over 50 runs alongside the stricken vessel in severe sea conditions, the lifeboat under his command sustained only minimal damage.'

Within 24 hours the *Ice Prince* disappeared under the waves, distributing her cargo of wood across the beaches of the south-west.

In 2009 a memorial to lifeboat men who have died on duty, which which is on page 17 of this book, was unveiled outside the RNLI headquarters in Poole. A taut steel figure urgently reaches out from a boat to someone struggling in the sea. The RNLI Heritage Trust chose a design by Sam Holland as that best representing the work of the charity.

On a plinth below the sculpture the names of 778 men are etched as a poignant reminder of their courage and sacrifice. Among the names are those of eight crew members of the steam lifeboat *James Stevens No. 4* who died in 1900 as she was leaving Padstow harbour.

Padstow's first lifeboat, named *Mariner's Friend,* was owned by the harbour association and was in action from 1827. By 1855, when the RNLI took over the lifeboat station at Padstow, the *Friend* was deemed 'unworthy of repairs' and replaced. A dozen years later five Padstow lifeboat men drowned when their boat capsized, including coxswain and three-time silver medal winner Daniel Shea.

There must have been hopes that the steam lifeboat, bought in 1899 at a cost of £3,340 and named after a Birmingham businessman who financed 20 lifeboats, would relegate tragedies like this to the past. But on 11 April 1900 the boat was overturned in a heavy swell and

sank while on her way to help fellow lifeboat men stranded on rocks nearby after their pulling boat *Arab* was swept away during a rescue. Only three crew members aboard the steam lifeboat survived, while those on the *Arab* managed to clamber to safety.

Those that died were coxswain David Grubb, John Bate, James Grubb, Edward Kane, John S. Martin, James B. Old, Joseph Stephens and Sydney East and they are remembered in a memorial in Padstow cemetery.

Unusually, perhaps, Padstow people kept the faith with new technology and from 1901 a steam tug called *Helen Peele* was kept in the estuary and used for pulling the oared lifeboat, *2nd Arab*. Although commandeered during the First World War, the tug remained in service in Padstow until 1929, the same year the tug's master Joseph Atkinson received a bronze medal for rescuing five crew from a wrecked fishing boat.

In 1931 *2nd Arab* was replaced by the *John and Sarah Eliza Stych*, which was on the station for seven years before transferring to St Ives, where it was wrecked in the 1939 disaster.

In August 1944 the sea off Padstow was thick with bodies after the Liberty ship *Ezra* and the Canadian corvette *Regina* were torpedoed by a U-boat in short order. The Liberty ship was holed first and it was wrongly reported that a stray mine was to blame. When the Canadian ship stopped to pick up survivors, it was torpedoed and sunk in less than a minute, with the loss of 30 lives.

The ships were part of a convoy, and other craft were soon on the scene to retrieve survivors from the water. However, they had been swiftly smothered in oil from the wrecks, and many others needed urgent medical attention following the explosions.

When the survivors were landed at Padstow – less than seven miles from the sinking – lifeboat men were perplexed and even angry at not

Above: The RNLI lifeguards at Woolacombe beach rescue a number of people washed out to see by the strong undercurrent.

Overleaf: The wreck of Padstow lifeboat *John and Sarah Eliza Stych* in 1939. Only one of the eight crew survived.

being involved in the rescue. Instantly, the lifeboat launched in a hunt for more survivors and brought some casualties picked up by other ships in the convoy back to shore, replenishing them with rum, biscuits and corned beef. In the lifeboat's log, however, the angry coxswain noted: 'I cannot understand why the services of the lifeboat were not utilised at 10.15 on the 8th instead of 12.30 on the 9th. Apparently over 100 men had been taken aboard a landing craft before the lifeboat was sent out to search for men in the sea.'

Later the same month there was another gripe recorded by the lifeboat crew, this time about changing naval communication frequencies. After a fruitless search for a naval ship the lifeboat log records: 'It would appear [the Royal Navy] have altered their wave length without notifying the lifeboat authority'.

As if to underline the difference the lifeboat men felt they could make during wartime, second motor mechanic William Orchard of Padstow was given a silver medal for his role in rescuing seven men from the Norwegian steamer *Sjofna* on 23 November 1944. Laden with a cargo of porcelain clay and heading for Northern Ireland, the *Sjofna* had run aground at Morwenstow, near Knap Head in North Devon, after detaching from a convoy.

Padstow's lifeboat on duty that day was the *Princess Mary*, and she battled 28 miles up the coast to the scene of the disaster. Lifeboats from Appledore and Clovelly were already there, but it was from the Padstow boat that a line was sent to the ship, which led to seven crew men being saved.

From land Hartland's rocket brigade then attached a line to the ship, although not at the first attempt. One rocket went through the window of the wheelhouse, breaking the captain's leg and briefly setting fire to the ship's cat. Despite that initial mishap the remaining 12 people, as well as the outraged cat, got to shore on a breeches

buoy. A witness to the lifeboat rescue that day was an Admiral Franklin, who according to the lifeboat logbook 'expressed high praise for the splendid seamanship'.

In 2006 a new lifeboat house was built at Padstow for a new lifeboat. The *Spirit of Padstow* is a Tamar class boat that is launched via the station's slipway. Seven crew man the boat, which is more than 16 metres long. It can achieve its top speed of 25 knots in about 25 seconds.

Tamar class lifeboats are equipped with state-of-the-art electronic systems that enable the crew to monitor the progress of the boat from the safety of their seats. It carries comprehensive first aid equipment, including oxygen, and even has an inflatable 'daughter' boat with a 15 horsepower engine that can be launched to operate in shallow seas when conditions allow. Below deck there's an area specially designated for survivors, with belted seats. Each boat costs £2.7 million – but to anyone involved in an emergency at sea it certainly feels like money well spent when that boat comes into view.

A second line of defence against casualties at sea was introduced by the RNLI in 2001. Lifeguards were posted on beaches, first in the south-west and later across the country. Just two years later a lifeguard won a bronze medal from the RNLI for his bravery in rescuing a swimmer. Rod MacDonald was off duty when he spotted a swimmer in difficulty off Fistral beach in Newquay. Without life-saving equipment to hand, he swam out to retrieve a man who had suffered a head injury and was in shock after being swept out to sea.

As training became key to its success, the RNLI opened the Lifeboat College in Poole in 2004. The first of its kind in the world, it manages to replicate the worst conditions at sea within the confines of a swimming pool.

Most of the time the pool looks like any other, although the water isn't warm. A platform above it at the height of a boat's side means that Lifeboat College students know what it would be like if they had to drop into the water in an emergency. When instructors want to simulate a storm, the blackout blinds are drawn and the wave machine is turned on. In addition, there are deafening sound effects like those of a low-flying helicopter, thunderclaps and a howling gale. Huddled inside an RIB, or inflatable life raft, the trainee crew learns what it is like to be in an emergency at night in terrible conditions. Apart from a rising tide of

Above: Rod MacDonald, who won a bronze medal from the RNLI for saving the life of an injured swimmer.

fear, the students must learn to combat a wave of seasickness that often accompanies this training session. And that's not all. There's sufficient space to practise capsizing. Crews learn what it will feel like if the ILB or raft they are using overturns, leaving them beneath it.

On the dry side, the Lifeboat College offers an equally stomach-churning experience in a wheelhouse simulator. Arrayed in front of the trainee are banks of controls just like those on a lifeboat. And out of the 'windows' ahead and to each side successive emergencies are digitally depicted. The trainee must think fast as he or she prioritises on a series of rescues. All the while the 'horizon' is moving much as it would in a rough sea.

The special effects are so realistic that it is difficult to believe this corner of the college is still very much on dry land. It's largely because of these extraordinary innovations that lifeboat crew are competent in all manner of emergencies. Crews come from all four nations and, thanks to the rigorous approach of the Lifeboat College, get excellent and uniform training.

Below: Getting to grips with capsizing at the Lifeboat College in Poole.

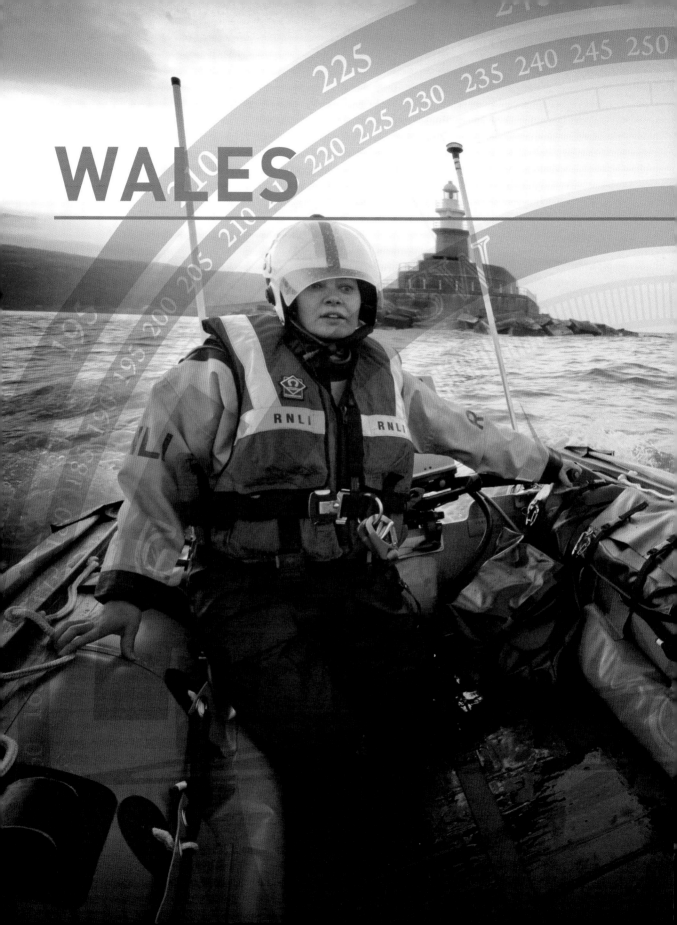

WALES

The middle of the 19th century saw lifeboat design once again become an incendiary topic. Unwittingly, the Duke of Northumberland lit the fuse in 1851 when he offered substantial prize money for the best lifeboat design. The detonation occurred when a boat submitted by Beeching, the eventual prize winner, was not deemed the best entry by those outside the judging panel, with seafarers everywhere having very certain opinions about what was right. Shock waves continued for months.

In Wales a father-and-son team had high hopes of victory for their tubular design which, they felt sure, outstripped others by a considerable margin. Henry Richardson, an officer in the Dragoon Guards during the Napoleonic Wars, had retired to Bala in North Wales, where he devoted his time to the issue of sea safety.

Together with his guardsman son, also called Henry, he drew up designs for the tubular lifeboat, which to the uneducated eye looked cumbersome, even comical. More raft than boat, it was pulled with 16 or 18 oars and had the capacity for sail. It was indeed difficult to manoeuvre at sea and certainly would never right itself. Yet the 33-foot long cork-clad boat was surprisingly light and buoyant. Its tubular framework was constructed in laminated wood, with each tube divided into watertight compartments.

Moreover, representing a departure from accepted lifeboat design principles, it had a grating rather than a floor and could function in extremely shallow water even when it was fully loaded. This ability was once demonstrated on a children's paddling pool in a park in Rhyl. The grating meant it could never be swamped with water – as water rushed in, so it went out again through the slats – although lifeboat men in the tubular models expected to get wetter than their counterparts in other boats.

Competition judges did not share the Richardsons' view. Outraged, and determined to prove the worth of their boat, father and son issued a public challenge, proposing competitive sea trials. In a letter intended for publication in *The Times*, the Richardsons wrote: 'If England wants real lifeboats, let practical trials be made before competent judges, and there would be some hope that the object might be attained and sterling boats established. It is melancholy that the interests of the many in this first of maritime nations should be made subservient to the opinions

Above: Tubular Class lifeboat *Morgan*, in service at Rhyl 1856–93.

of the few on a subject of such vital importance and which ought and shortly must call for the attention of Parliament.'

The Times declined to publish the letter, perhaps because the Richardsons had begun to call established designs 'death boats' as part of a continuing tirade. They were also free with insults towards Captain John Ward, the Chief Inspector of Lifeboats, whose task it was to defend serving lifeboats. (He was also the designer of cork life jackets and spent more than 30 years in post.)

Now their tubular lifeboat, constructed in Manchester and suitably named the *Challenger*, was taken on a tour from Liverpool to Ramsgate in the hope of persuading coastal towns of its merits. Intent though the Richardsons were on establishing their lifeboat, they were not above playing bizarre practical jokes. When the *Challenger* appeared suddenly out of fog at Lytham in Lancashire, the crew spoke in French and fired a brass swivel gun aboard.

'The effect was prodigious,' they later wrote. 'All fled like a flock of frightened sheep, shouting that a French lugger had landed . . . These occurrences gave us the idea of procuring masks, which

appendages on our voyage around the coast of Wales caused much terror. We procured a set of masks of differing degrees of ferocity and ugliness – a boar's head with tremendous tusks, a nose a foot long with a French red cap, a devil's mask, a crocodile's head and others . . . Pilots and all fled from us.'

Whether or not such japes helped the Richardsons' campaign, soon a disaster at sea did offer support to their argument. On 22 January 1853, the Rhyl lifeboat *Seagull*, drawn up to James Beeching's design and operated by the Shipwrecked Fishermen and Mariners Benevolent Society, sank with the loss of six crew men. The lifeboat had been called out to the rescue of a ship in the vicinity. But by the time the lifeboat arrived the casualty had disappeared – it had probably already fallen victim to an incoming tide. The *Seagull* then got into trouble as it headed for home.

Coxswain Owen Jones later described what happened. 'The boat in going on the top of a heavy broken sea broached to a little as the sea left her bows and made a heavy lurch to the leeward and took some water over the gunwale. She then lurched to windward and the sea broke on her. She then completely capsized and turned bottom up.'

The coxswain and one other got in the boat, which had righted herself, and lassoed another man who was then towed into shore. By now they were so numb with cold they could barely help one another. Jones threw out oars to other crew, hoping they would provide buoyancy. But all who remained in the sea drowned, their bodies washed up on Welsh beaches in subsequent days.

As it turned out, Richardson had good grounds in this instance for holding up his design above Beeching's, given the specific conditions around Rhyl. The tubular lifeboat was in fact ideal for the soft banking sands around the beaches of North Wales and the Dee estuary. One tubular lifeboat, the *Morgan*, consequently did sterling service at Rhyl between 1856 and 1893. A second tubular boat, the *Caroline Richardson II*, operated out of Rhyl from its arrival in 1897 to the start of the Second World War, by which time it was affectionately known as 'the banana boat'. It launched 17 times and saved 10 lives. From 1878 a second lifeboat station was established at Rhyl, housing a self-righting lifeboat.

The *Challenger*, the Richardsons' original boat, was sold to the Portuguese to operate in Oporto. Another was installed at New

Opposite: Tubular lifeboat in Rhyl.

Overleaf: Trearddur Bay Atlantic 85 inshore lifeboat *Hereford Endeavour.*

Brighton in Merseyside, where it was an asset, well suited to the sandy conditions of the estuary nearby.

Another type of lifeboat rarely seen on service in the UK was a familiar sight at Holyhead in Anglesey. Steam power had been in the ascendancy over sail for a long time before the Institution was persuaded to use it. Indeed, Sir William Hillary had advocated steam power when the Institution was established, and there were some steam-powered entries in the 1851 lifeboat design competition.

But nay-sayers who considered steam too unorthodox always won the day. As late as the 1870s, an RNLI committee looking once again at the possibility of steam power reported that it 'did not feel able to expect that steam lifeboats will ever come into general use'.

With steam came two major disadvantages. It took time to get up a head of steam, delaying response to an emergency. Also, stokers needed to work non-stop in stormy conditions to keep consistent power – even while being tossed around the engine-room as the boat tipped and rolled with the waves. What would happen to men and machinery if the boat overturned and righted itself? Furthermore, steam lifeboats had to be kept in deeper seas, as their machinery below the waterline could be damaged in the shallows.

In total six steam lifeboats wore RNLI livery, the first being the *Duke of Northumberland*, which spent two years in service at Harwich and underwent exhaustive trials before coming to Holyhead in 1892. Soon afterwards she was stationed at New Brighton, on the Wirral, for a short spell before returning to Holyhead for 25 years' unbroken service. She was 50 feet long and could travel at nine knots thanks to her water turbine. During that quarter-century she was launched 125 times and saved 239 lives, most memorably from the SS *Harold*, wrecked off Anglesey in 1908.

The *Harold* had been bound for Runcorn, on the Mersey, from Teignmouth, in South Devon, with a cargo of china clay when it ran into violent winds and high seas. A passing ship that witnessed its plight tried to send over a tow line, but all efforts came to nothing owing to the storm. Only its anchor was holding the *Harold* a whisker away from obliteration on the rocky coast.

When the lifeboat arrived at the scene after battling through the waves for two hours, coxswain William Owen realised that the

combination of the heavy weather and the *Harold*'s proximity to the rocks made a rescue attempt too dangerous.

Patiently he waited for two hours until the tide turned, bringing about a short period of slack water. Then he worked fast. A line was at last sent over to the *Harold* and seven of nine crew men were pulled back along it, washed down by waves as they did so.

Before the final two could be liberated from the *Harold* a huge wave bore down on the *Duke of Northumberland* and carried it towards the ship. A devastating collision seemed inevitable. However, the wave passed on, leaving the lifeboat close enough to the casualty for the men to jump aboard while Owen held the boat steady.

The lifeboat returned to Holyhead, with everyone aboard convinced that an oared lifeboat would have been lost with all hands in the attempt. In recognition of their achievement the ten crew of the *Duke of Northumberland* were awarded silver RNLI gallantry medals, while the coxswain won gold.

Two other lifeboats with the same hydraulic pumps to power them were the *City of Glasgow*, which operated out of Harwich and Gorleston, and the *Queen*, at New Brighton.

Steam lifeboat design evolved quickly, with water jets replacing the turbine. The three lifeboats that completed the complement of six were the *James Stevens No. 3*, which had a varied career including spells at Dover and Holyhead, the *James Stevens No. 4*, wrecked at Padstow, and the *City of Glasgow II*, which served Harwich. However, thanks to its belated arrival in the RNLI fleet, steam was soon yesterday's technology. With the 20th century came the advent of the motorised boat, which was lighter, cheaper and more versatile than steamers.

The First World War brought grief to small communities all across the country, but for lifeboat men who continually risked their lives there was little distinction to be drawn between times of conflict and peace. When the small coastal town of Port Eynon was enveloped by grief, for example, it was the sea rather than the enemy that was to blame.

A lifeboat station had been established at Port Eynon in 1883, after residents watched in horror as the crew of the *Agnes Jack* perished, out of range of the rocket equipment swiftly brought to the scene. Lloyd's agent Charles Bevan recorded the scene:

Opposite: Porthcawl crew volunteers on exercise in a 20-feet deep crevice at Box Bay.

By this time scores of men had arrived but nothing could be done to rescue the men from their perilous position. The wind blew with terrific force, and the sea was frightful to look at. Huge waves rolled in one after another, breaking on the rocks, the foam and spray rising in the air like clouds. Every eye was fixed on the frail mast to which the doomed sailors clung, and every moment was expected to be the last. At about nine o'clock one of the men was seen to fall into the sea and disappear. The other poor fellows appeared to be stripping themselves of their clothes, one thing after another, boots &co were seen dropping into the sea, as if the men were preparing to swim. Then a man was seen going down hand over hand. He paused a moment and then plunged into the water, and struck out for the shore, but was soon lost sight of. About ten o'clock the Rhossili brigade arrived, and more rockets were fired, but to no effect. Shortly after ten, a tremendous wave struck the mast, and it fell carrying with it about ten precious souls. From five to seven heads were visible above water for a few minutes, swimming hard for shore. They succeeded in getting about thirty yards from the wreck when they were all lost sight of except for one, who was very near the rocks, but the rebound of the sea took him off again. It was a heart-rending sight to behold – a sight that will never be forgotten by those who witnessed it.'

Above: Porthcawl lifeboat rescues a couple who had been cut off by the tide for 24 hours.

The dead were mostly from Wales, as the ship had set out from The Mumbles, in Glamorganshire, only an hour before it ran into difficulties. It didn't take much to persuade the RNLI that a lifeboat station was needed. A local man gave land for a lifeboat house, and a Liverpool woman paid for the house to be built and for the boat,

named *A Daughter's Offering*, to go inside. The lifeboat was kept busy before being replaced in 1906 with a new one called the *Janet*.

A decade later, at the midpoint of the global conflict, the lifeboat overturned twice after being called out to help SS *Dunvegan*, whose crew were ultimately saved via rocket apparatus. The *Janet* was making for home when powerful waves turned her over and three men failed to resurface. Left with only three oars, the remaining crew – including two servicemen home on leave – were compelled to put down the anchor and spend the night sheltering as best they could from the terrible weather.

By the following morning the lifeboat had drifted to The Mumbles, where the men were finally hauled ashore and given medical attention before being dispatched home by bus. Soon afterwards the lifeboat station was closed. Victims coxswain Billy Gibbs (whose body was never found), William Eynon and his brother-in-law George Harry are recalled by an impressive marble statue of a lifeboat man at St Cattwg's Church in Port Eynon.

Fortunately, the areas offshore of Swansea and the Gower peninsula were still well served, and it was here that the holed Canadian frigate *Chebogue* came to grief in 1944. The frigate was picked off in mid-Atlantic by a U-boat while on convoy duty, but hobbled back to Britain towed by various ships. Having survived a direct hit, those aboard were relieved to see the Welsh coast within touching distance when the anchor was dropped on 11 October. However, a ferocious storm was brewing which uprooted the anchor and sent the disabled ship scudding across the bay, until it lodged on a sandbar.

As the Mumbles lifeboat was launched, the crew knew it was a notoriously difficult area in which to accomplish a rescue. Crew member Charlie Davies was a survivor of a disaster there in 1903 in which six Mumbles lifeboat men drowned when the *James Stevens No. 14* capsized.

HAVING SURVIVED A DIRECT HIT, THOSE ABOARD WERE RELIEVED TO SEE THE WELSH COAST WITHIN TOUCHING DISTANCE

The *Edward, Prince of Wales* was a 45-foot Watson class powered by a single 80-horsepower petrol engine and had been robust in service since its delivery from boat-builders J.S. White of Cowes. It was bought in 1924 at a cost of £12,800.

Without dwelling on the difficulties that lay ahead, the men took the motorised lifeboat into the night through a perpetual shower of seawater. It was not a night for a rescue by ropes or breeches buoy. When they located the frigate they decided to take the crew off by running alongside, close enough for men to jump. Coxswain William Gammon veered around the ship a dozen times, collecting three or four men each time. Each time the lifeboat risked being smashed by the lurching *Chebogue*.

Still, 42 men were rescued with minimal injuries. One man broke a leg as he dropped into the lifeboat from the deck of the frigate. Another man fell between the boats but was hauled to safety by willing hands and suffered no more than a soaking. A third had his fall broken by Coxswain Gammon, who was badly bruised.

It took 90 minutes to complete the rescue, after which the grateful frigate crew were returned to The Mumbles. In his report of the incident the naval commander at Swansea wrote: 'The commanding officer and all his men were unanimous in their admiration of the splendid way in which the lifeboat was handled by Coxswain Gammon and say that the whole crew were magnificent.'

Afterwards Gammon was awarded a gold medal for conspicuous gallantry, with mechanic William Davies and bowman Thomas Ace each receiving a bronze. Other crew members were given the Thanks of the Institution inscribed on vellum.

Two of the men were in their seventies and a further two were in their sixties, lifeboat men being in short supply in wartime.

Once again, history was determined to illustrate that joyful success was only a heartbeat away from tearful tragedy. On 23 April 1947, Gammon and Davies were among eight lifeboat men from The Mumbles who died trying to save the crew of the liberty ship *Samtamper*, beached on shallow coastal ledges.

Conditions were treacherous when the lifeboat launched. No one knows what happened in the final moments of the lifeboat and her crew, as the men of the *Samtamper* who were perhaps witnesses were

Above: Coxswain William Gammon.

Opposite: The rescue of the crew of the *Chebogue*.

all lost too. In addition to Gammon and Davies, the lifeboat men who died were second coxswain William Noel, second mechanic Ernest Griffin, bowman William Thomas, William Howell, Ronald Thomas and Richard Smith.

Still, catastrophes like these did not deter lifeboat men of Wales, including the legendary Richard Evans. At the time of the tragedy at The Mumbles, Evans was 42 years old and had yet to become coxswain in his home town of Moelfre, Anglesey. It was also before he won either of his two gold medals for bravery – Evans was one of only five lifeboat men to achieve a pair of golds. Lifeboats were in his blood, as his father, uncle and two grandfathers all served in the Moelfre crew. Later his three sons, David, Derek and William, joined him in the lifeboat.

Richard Evans – better known as Dick – had originally planned a life at sea, far away from Moelfre, becoming a cabin boy on a coaster at the age of 14 and graduating to master mariner by the age of 23. But when his uncle John Matthews left the family butcher's shop to become full-time lifeboat coxswain, Evans was recalled to take his place behind the counter. At least he could work as bowman on the lifeboat, at the time still powered by oar and sail.

During the Second World War he became second coxswain and was also signal sergeant in the Home Guard platoon. Evans won his first medal, a bronze, for his part in the rescue of three airmen from a crashed Whitley bomber.

In 1954 he became lifeboat coxswain. Five years later, on the centenary of the wreck of the *Royal Charter* nearby, Evans took the reserve lifeboat *Edmund and Mary Robinson* to the aid of the *Hindlea*. A comparatively small boat, the *Hindlea* was being tossed around Moelfre Bay in hurricane winds and was only yards from the rocks by the time the lifeboat arrived.

Evans was short-handed, and one of the crew members, Hugh

Jones, had never been to sea in the lifeboat before. As the *Hindlea* pitched in the heaving waves, her propellers thrashed in the air and risked slicing into lifeboat and crew as she came by.

Nonetheless, Evans made ten runs at the rolling craft, picking up a crew man on each occasion. The lifeboat toiled through 30-foot waves to return to its base and launched for a second time just 45 minutes later to attend another emergency. Evans was awarded a gold medal and his mechanic Evan Owens a silver. The other crew members, Donald 'Murley' Francis, Hugh Owen and Hugh Jones, were given bronze medals.

Evans won his second gold medal at the age of 61 for his role in rescuing the crew of a Greek freighter, *Nafsiporos*, on 2 December 1966. Mechanic Evan Owens recalled the night:

> It was a night when lifeboat men are uneasy, thinking of the storm and of the many things that can cause a distress call. As I listened to the roof slates rattling in the gale at Lifeboat House, the howling kept me awake thinking of those men out at sea. I had been one myself for many years.
>
> At 6 a.m. Dick Evans the coxswain rang. He had received a message from Holyhead that the motor vessel *Vinland* had engine failure 20 miles north of Point Lynas and required assistance, a tug if possible, so would we stand by to launch if a call should come? I opened my back door and closed it quickly, as the cast-iron gutters came crashing down. The village was lit up by flashes as the overhead electricity cables shorted. Everything movable was blowing around wildly and chimney pots and slates crashed down. Every experienced lifeboat man knows the feeling; one just knows it is going to happen.

Left: The wreck of the *Hindlea*. Coxswain Dick Evans was awarded a gold medal for his part in the rescue of her crew.

There were a succession of casualties needing attention, and it took in the order of six hours to attend to them all. And the moment the lifeboat *Watkin Williams* returned to base was the instant they were asked to go to Holyhead – a grinding, lengthy voyage in conditions like these.

Moelfre's lifeboat was not the only one heading for the north-west tip of Anglesey, where the 1,287-ton *Nafsiporos* was foundering. Lifeboats from the Isle of Man and Holyhead had the same target in their sights. Only a lifeboat would do. Attempts made by a passing Soviet ship and an RAF helicopter to help had come to nothing.

Holyhead's lifeboat got to the freighter first but was badly damaged in the process of coming alongside. When it pulled away it was the turn of the Moelfre lifeboat. By now the Isle of Man lifeboat had returned to base.

Later Evans said: 'I knew the rocks, the set and drift of the tides, the currents. But that day the sea was like a foreign country. With the leaping and plunging of the lifeboat the compass was swinging wildly. I could see nothing. The sea was being blown into clouds of spray and visibility was nil. We had to run on dead reckoning.'

Each tumultuous wave threatened to put the lifeboats into a spin. Then Evans realised his boat was dipping. The sea had forced its way through two deck ventilators and the bow was full of water. He dispatched his son and a crew member to investigate. Still, Evans decided to continue with an approach to the flailing vessel. The terrified crew followed the lifeboat with their eyes as it went high then dived with the force of the waves. None would venture near the exit ladder, which was swinging wildly.

Holyhead's boat circled once more, with RNLI inspector Harold Harvey at the helm as coxswain Thomas Alcock went forward to help haul frightened men to safety. Five men were enticed or manhandled to safety before the wrecked vessel's lifeboat crashed down on to the RNLI boat, as if to emphasise the danger they were in. By a miracle, no one was injured.

Now Evans came forward again, and this time ten men got into his boat with the help of the lifeboat crew. Four men refused to leave, however.

Concerned for the welfare of those already saved, the lifeboats set a course for Holyhead. By the time they landed, the Moelfre crew had

THE TERRIFIED CREW FOLLOWED THE LIFEBOAT WITH THEIR EYES AS IT WENT HIGH THEN DIVED WITH THE FORCE OF THE WAVES

been in action for 23 hours without food. Evans had been at the helm for an uninterrupted 12-hour stint. This time it was the Holyhead boat that turned about. It stood by as a Dutch tug finally succeeded in attaching a tow line, saving the ship and the remaining crew.

Alongside Evans, Inspector of Lifeboats Harold Harvey was awarded the gold medal. There were silver medals for Alcock and mechanics Eric Jones of Holyhead and Evan Owens of Moelfre, and bronze medals for the rest of the crews. Evans was also awarded the British Empire Medal in 1969, and was seen on television. He was a subject for *This Is Your Life* and appeared on Michael Parkinson's chat show.

When Evans retired in 1970 he had an impressive set of statistics to his name. Since joining as a 16-year-old he had helped launch the lifeboat 179 times and saved 281 lives. He then became a fundraiser for the RNLI, travelling around the country to give talks about his experiences in a lifeboat. When he spoke at the 150th anniversary celebration of the RNLI he was given a standing ovation.

After he died, aged 96, his coffin was lowered into the ground to the sound of the maroons which had once called him into perilous action.

Below: New Quay D class inshore lifeboat *Amy Lea*, in service since 2004.

Lifeboat men in Wales have tackled all kinds of dramas at sea. On 17 September 1962, the Rhyl lifeboat became the first to deal with a hovercraft emergency. The hovercraft had been moored at Rhyl after a summer season ferrying people across the River Dee. When a vicious storm blew in, three crew members tried to take the hovercraft out to sea in search of safety, but the driving waves were too strong for the lightweight craft. Coxswain Harold Campini brought the Rhyl lifeboat *Anthony Robert Marshall* alongside the hovercraft, which was now drifting at the mercy of the elements, and the three crew men jumped aboard minutes before it hit the promenade. Aboard there were 250 gallons of fuel, enough to cause a major inferno. Shore helpers risked their lives to secure the hovercraft to the promenade to prevent this happening. Coxswain Campini won the silver medal for gallantry and crew members got vellum certificates. The courage of the shore team was recognised with letters of thanks.

In August 2004 on the coast of South Wales, a severe storm was battering a stranded fishing vessel. Aileen Jones, who received the bronze medal for gallantry for the rescue, was part of a small team that skilfully towed the stricken *Gower Pride* to safety, overcoming complications and malfunctions in torrid conditions.

There were two men on board, one of them injured. They had thrown down two anchors, but these were not holding as powerful swells and huge waves rocked the vulnerable ship. After crew member Simon Emms replaced a broken tow line, Jones, 41 at the time, carefully manoeuvred the two vessels apart and began a slow tow to safety.

'I have been a part of many rescues, but this was the one that stands out in my mind. The sea was so rough, and it was in August so we didn't expect what we faced,' said Jones, who was working as a volunteer alongside her job as a nurse at a nursery. 'We knew it would be hard, but we didn't have time to be scared because the adrenalin kicks in. To us, it was just another job.'

The training automatically took over as each of them figured out what they were going to do. 'We discussed it between ourselves and we each had in our minds how we would tackle the situation. I, as helmsman, knew what I needed to achieve.'

Although proud of her medal, Jones was quick to praise her co-workers. 'Team work is so important during situations like we were facing. We all rely on each other and it is the most important attribute when working at the RNLI.'

Brought up on the coast, Jones had always wanted to be involved in the organisation in one way or another. 'When I was younger I knew somebody who worked at the RNLI and whenever I could I would join in with the crew, but I was probably just a nuisance.'

She believes that, as an organisation, it does more than just save lives. 'The RNLI are the heart of the community. It's an organisation that teaches young and old people about sea safety and welcomes volunteers. We come from all walks of life. I work in a school, others have jobs as postmen and builders. We are all brought together by the RNLI and it has a wonderful atmosphere.'

Despite working on scary rescue operations, Jones maintains her worst fear lies in the training. 'I hated being underneath the boat during capsize drills. I didn't like having my head submerged under water with a helmet on. These were the only times that I was scared during my time in the RNLI.'

Overleaf: Kate Middleton and Prince William launch the new *Hereford Endeavour* lifeboat in March 2011 at Trearddur Bay Lifeboat Station in Anglesey.

NORTH-WEST

IRISH SEA

As the path of a distress rocket split the night sky above Lytham, not one but three lifeboats prepared for action. Saving the lives of the sailors on the German barque *Mexico* was the sole objective of the men as they pulled on oilskins and braced themselves for the hard labour of rowing through a heavy swell. None spared a thought for personal safety as they thrust the lifeboats into wintry seas heading for treacherous estuary waters. As it turned out, only one of the trio of boats would return, hours later, after a heavy sea had wreaked havoc.

Thomas Clarkson, the coxswain of the Lytham boat which came back unscathed with the crew of the wrecked ship, described at an inquest what his men had faced on the night of 9 December 1886. 'There was a gale of wind blowing. The sea near Southport was very high and, shortly before getting to the ship, it was mountains high. Sometimes it was breaking, sometimes it was not. In its course it was running all one way. On the bank the water was properly broken.'

He told how difficult it was to find the ship in the dark, how four oars snapped when seawater broke over their boat, how a black box containing the ship's papers was lost to the sea bottom during the drama.

Nevertheless the rescue was a success. Men from the Hamburg-registered boat slithered down its sides on ropes to the relative safety of the lifeboat *Charles Biggs*, only recently arrived at Lytham after being an exhibit at the Liverpool International Exhibition and that night earning its first colours.

As the rescue was taking place, the men on the *Mexico* and the lifeboat men of Lytham had no idea that lifeboats from nearby St Anne's and from Southport had also put to sea. Men in the Lytham lifeboat were only dimly aware of crowds gathering in the gloom at the front in Southport and didn't realise they were grimly waiting for a sign from the town's lifeboat.

It was the following morning before the jubilant people of Lytham realised what had happened, when a telegram arrived telling of the disaster. Immediately the *Charles Biggs* was launched in a vain search for survivors.

There was no one left alive from the *Laura Janet* of St Anne's, which was found the following day upturned on the banks of the Ribble estuary with the bodies of three men trapped beneath, so it is

AS THE RESCUE WAS TAKING PLACE, THE MEN ON THE *MEXICO* AND THE LIFEBOAT MEN OF LYTHAM HAD NO IDEA THAT LIFEBOATS FROM NEARBY ST ANNE'S AND FROM SOUTHPORT HAD ALSO PUT TO SEA

impossible to know what occurred. If it had capsized, the boat should have self-righted and offered some hope for the crew.

A silver watch belonging to one of the dead stopped at 2.20 a.m., which indicated that the men of the *Laura Janet* had battled against the storm for some hours before succumbing.

Two men survived from the Southport crew of the *Eliza Fernley*. A third, who was alive when he reached the shore, died soon afterwards in hospital. The testimony given within 24 hours of the tragedy by survivor John Jackson, whose brother died unseen but only yards away from him, provided some information about what had happened. The Southport crew had been observing the unsteady progress of the *Mexico* and were prepared to launch.

> At last signals of distress were observed; the barque, evidently standing nearer shore, sent up rockets and flashed lights for help. Captain Hodge [the coxswain] lost no time in getting

Above: Hoylake Mersey class all-weather lifeboat *Lady of Hilbre* makes a splash.

Overleaf: Lytham lifeboat *Charles Biggs* with the men that went to the wreck of the *Mexico* and rescued her crew of 12.

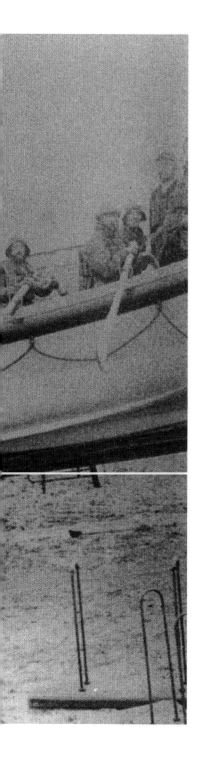

the boat out. At ten minutes to ten the horses set off with the boat and, after experiencing considerable difficulty, we launched the boat at 11 p.m. A large crowd saw us off and the excitement was tremendous. The boat was launched successfully and went nicely for a time.

Unknown to the crew of the *Mexico*, the Southport men had fought hard to get within 30 yards of the ship. As they positioned themselves to go to the ship, their lifeboat was turned upside down by a mammoth wave.

We expected her to right herself but she remained bottom upwards. Some of us managed at length to crawl out. I and Richard Robinson held firmly on to the rowlocks and were buffeted about considerably.

With some difficulty I got underneath the boat again and spoke, I think, to Henry Robinson, Thomas Jackson, Timothy Rigby and Peter Jackson. I called out, 'I think she will never right; we have all to be drowned.' I heard a voice – I think it was Henry Robinson's – say, 'I think so too.' I got out again and found Richard Robinson fairly done. He leaned heavily on my arm and I think he must have been suffocated. Another sea came, and when it receded he had disappeared and I never saw him again. While underneath I called out to my brother, 'Clasper' – that is a sort of nickname we gave him – but I could get no answer.

The boat eventually drifted bottom upwards to the shore and those who were rescued, like myself, clung to her. … I never saw any of the other lifeboats.'

The other survivor, Henry Robinson, had two brothers aboard. As Christmas approached, the loss of 17 RNLI men to the sea on a single night provoked an outpouring of grief across Victorian England. A fund was established to support the 16 widows created by the disaster and their 50 children. In a matter of weeks it had raised £30,000.

There was speculation that the lifeboats were not equal to the conditions. *The Times* thundered: 'What a scandal to intelligence and humanity that brave men should be persuaded to risk their lives in

boats so unsuitable for their work as the Southport and St Anne's must have been. Had a tithe of the ingenuity and capital devoted to the improvement of torpedoes been expended on improving lifeboats, how different would have been their condition.'

In response the RNLI reported that for 32 years the self-righting lifeboats had been launched almost 5,000 times and saved more than 12,000 lives. Boats that capsized tended to right themselves, with lives lost on only 18 previous occasions, accounting for the deaths of 76 lifeboat men. That, said the RNLI, represented one in every 850 lifeboat men involved.

Ultimately it is thought the Southport boat failed to right itself because, according to Jackson, the anchor had already been cast down and was perhaps pinning it into position. Men clinging to the boat might also have hampered the righting action. Meanwhile the St Anne's boat possibly overturned in water too shallow to permit its rotation.

However, troubling revelations about the poor fitness of the St Anne's crew emerged. The coxswain, William Johnson, was severely weakened by tuberculosis. At least one crew member was under-nourished, being short of money and inclined to give the family's paltry supplies of food to his wife and children.

Statues were sculpted and memorials raised to the lost men. But the story became carved into the very soul of the coastal communities in the north-west, and even beyond. The deaths of the 27 were pivotal in Institution history.

The disaster of 1886 had far-reaching ramifications for RNLI fund-raising – and charitable causes across the board. Among the residents of St Anne's at the time was wealthy businessman Charles Macara, from Manchester. He believed the quiet seaside town would be a bolt-hole from the pressures of Victorian enterprise. He found himself content in the company of local fishermen and even went

Above: Blackpool Atlantic
75 and Lytham Mersey Class
are launched to a yacht with
two unwell crewmembers
onboard. Blackpool lifeboat
crew transfer the casualties
from the yacht to Lytham
ALB and they are returned
to shore.

out with them on fishing trips. And after the twin lifeboat losses in the north-west he found himself spearheading a new endeavour that spread throughout England.

Owning the only telephone in the town, on the night of the *Mexico* rescue Macara was at the heart of the drama, sending telegrams up and down the coast hoping for news of washed-up survivors. When the full scale of the disaster unfolded he shared the despair of those around him and resolved to make a difference.

When he investigated the Institution's finances he discovered that only a relatively small number of rich philanthropists – about 100 – were keeping it afloat. He believed it was time to spread the net wider, convinced it would garner more cash. He had in his sights the growing urban populations who, though far from the sea, were still struck by the raw courage of the lifeboat men. He had a bold plan for persuading them to contribute, and in July 1891 he began the groundwork for his appeal with an open letter to the British press.

I think the British public generally have very little idea that one of the noblest of the numerous philanthropic institutions in the country is in dire financial straits. The record of the Royal National Life-boat Institution since its formation is one of which the nation is justly proud, as by its instrumentality over 35,000 lives have been saved at sea, and the many deeds of heroism which have been chronicled in connection with its operations are the envy of the whole civilised world.

Having a seaside residence on one of the most dangerous parts of the Lancashire coast, I have had opportunities of witnessing the conspicuous gallantry of our Lifeboat men that do not fall to the lot of many. It has also been my painful experience to be prominently associated with the most terrible disaster that ever befell the Lifeboat service, when the whole of the St Anne's crew were swept away, and all but two of the brave men who manned the Southport boat returned no more.

The great power of the Press was never better illustrated than on that memorable occasion, as, mainly by the pathetic appeals that were made through it, considerably over £30,000 was raised for the widows and children of the drowned men. The late German Emperor, William I, was so much touched with this disaster that he sent £250 for distribution amongst the bereaved. Such a magnificent result has emboldened me to appeal once more by the same means to the public on behalf of this great national institution, which is sorely in need of funds. The deficit last year assumed alarming proportions, and unless the country is roused to supply the necessary means, the Institution's operations will be very seriously curtailed.

By October plans for the first ever 'Lifeboat Saturday' were poised to swing into action. Two reserve lifeboats and their crews were pulled on carriages through the streets of Manchester and Salford for two days before its inauguration.

On the day of the parade, lifeboat men in the boat were armed with long poles that had nets attached, so they could reach up to receive donations offered from high windows and the top decks of trams. The boat was accompanied by a phalanx of women collecting cash at ground level. A book about Macara written in 1917 contains the following description:

> The appointed day was processional, and culminated in the launching of the lifeboats at Belle Vue Gardens in the presence of 30,000 spectators. The fullest advantage was taken of Sir Charles Macara's organisation for collecting subscriptions and donations, and the city was dredged of its spare cash . . . at the end of the day Manchester and Salford, which had been contributing £200 per annum to the saving of life at sea, had given £5,500.
>
> 'Lifeboat Saturday' spread. By the end of 1893 it had become a feature of English life. It raised the annual average

LIFEBOAT MEN IN THE BOAT WERE ARMED WITH LONG POLES THAT HAD NETS ATTACHED, SO THEY COULD REACH UP TO RECEIVE DONATIONS OFFERED FROM HIGH WINDOWS AND THE TOP DECKS OF TRAMS

Opposite: The first Lifeboat Saturday event in Manchester in 1891.

income of the Royal National Lifeboat Institution directly
and indirectly by £40,000, thereby making it possible to
increase the remuneration of the lifeboat men. Incidentally it
revolutionised the methods of collecting money in England. It
brought charity into the streets and the streets into charity.
As the first of many consecrated 'Saturdays', it was the
beginning of a great humanisation of the common life by the
breath of generous causes.

Lady Marion Macara was also heavily involved in fund-raising for
the RNLI, establishing the first Ladies Auxiliary Group. Women who
joined groups like this did legwork on Lifeboat Saturdays alongside
the lifeboat men themselves, collecting cash and later dispensing
lifeboat emblems. They were the first in a long tradition of dedicated
tin-rattlers who have since haunted high streets of Britain.

The loss of the Southport and St Anne's lifeboat also led to
a review of the RNLI after it requested a parliamentary inquiry.
Following a disaster of such immense proportions, critics of the
organisation found themselves some willing listeners. Among
those who had the Institution in their sights was a former MP and
coachbuilder whose company's work had been rejected by it.

There was talk – sometimes based in truth – of lifeboat men
who plundered cargo from wrecks that should have been left to
the salvagers. One witness who spoke out against the Institution
at the inquiry was Macara, who was vexed by the way his slick
administration in the north-west had been hijacked by the head
office in London.

At the end of the thorough inquiry, in which 11,864 questions
were put to witnesses, a report running to more than 1,000 pages
largely exonerated the RNLI of wrong-doing. It found that when

lifeboat men had been guilty of taking goods from wrecks they were reprimanded or even dismissed. Every effort had been made to provide them with the best quality boats and equipment, contrary to the messages sent out by the slighted coachbuilder. Money from disaster funds was not being misappropriated, as had been claimed.

Once again the RNLI stood in the sun. It had regained the faith of the public and there were more local committees than ever before, reflecting a renewed well of support.

The north-west had a role to play in lifeboat design. Liverpool boat-builder Thomas Costain entered the Duke of Northumberland's competition in 1851. Although his model wasn't successful, aspects of its design were adopted subsequently by the RNLI. Buoyancy came from a leather-covered cork fender running the length of the lifeboat and airtight casks secured in wooden cases along the sides. There were a dozen oars, two spritsails and a jib. Costain built nine lifeboats of this type for the Liverpool Dock Board Trustees in 1840. They were used in Liverpool Bay, assisting 269 wrecks and saving 1,128 lives.

The RNLI defines itself proudly, simply and accurately as 'the charity that saves lives at sea'. Yet there are times, thankfully rare, when the challenge is beyond any crew; where skill and courage alone will never be enough to overcome the odds.

So it was on the dreadful night of 5 February 2004, when the treacherous sands of Morecambe Bay claimed the lives of 23 Chinese cockle pickers, a disaster that horrified the British public and sent shock waves around the world.

That these victims – men and women aged between 18 and 45, all illegal immigrants – were callously sent to a terrible death almost defies belief. They were driven on to Warton Sands on the orders of

Above: RNLI Hoylake lifeboat *Lady of Hilbre* and New Brighton inshore lifeboat *Charles Dibdin* rescue a 120-ton trawler aground on Taylors Bank in Liverpool Bay.

Right: The *Hurley Flyer* hovercraft at Morecambe Bay, which has its fair share of incidents thanks to the shifting sands and fast-moving tides.

29-year-old gangmaster Lin Liang Ren, even though a rough sea and deteriorating weather were keeping most other cockle pickers away. Here were poor, vulnerable people, from farming backgrounds in China, most of whom had never seen the sea until Lin Liang Ren signed them up.

During the gangmaster's trial – he later received a 14-year sentence for manslaughter – prosecutor Tim Holroyde QC summed up the hopelessness of their position: 'Far from home and unable to speak sufficient English to summon help, in the cold and dark, with no obvious route back to shore even if they could swim and with the water rising swiftly and inexorably.' Truly, this was the stuff of nightmares.

A small consolation for relatives was that almost all the bodies of their loved ones were recovered by the RNLI. The crews never sought sympathy or accolades for their horrendous duty that night, yet the lasting effect it had on them should not be underestimated. Given that media coverage understandably focused on the victims and their criminal masters, the crews' ordeal has perhaps never been fully acknowledged.

Few were better placed to judge the mental and physical challenge they faced than Michael Guy, then aged 60. As Morecambe RNLI's deputy launching authority he controlled the search operation from the shore, supervising the launch of the station's new hovercraft, the *Hurley Flyer,* and the 'D' class inshore lifeboat, the *Peter Bond.* As the scale of the tragedy became clear, Mr Guy realised that his experience as an NHS Registered Mental Nurse, which included treatment of post-traumatic disorders, was likely to prove as important to the team as any leadership skills he could offer.

> We faced a series of events which combined to make this rescue attempt particularly difficult [recalls Mr Guy]. It was a filthy night, the sea was rough, it was pitch black and the one man we did manage to bring to safety could only repeat the words 'many, many, many' as he struggled to explain what was happening.
>
> The cockle pickers were in an area close to where freshwater rivers enter the Bay. Those rivers were swollen from heavy rain, that water was much colder than the sea and the currents were fast. The effect would have been to

IN THE COLD AND DARK, WITH NO OBVIOUS ROUTE BACK TO SHORE EVEN IF THEY COULD SWIM AND WITH THE WATER RISING SWIFTLY AND INEXORABLY ... THIS WAS THE STUFF OF NIGHTMARES.

sweep you off your legs while at the same time an incoming
tide rolled over you. Morecambe Bay is basically 100
square miles of shifting, unstable sands and it is hard to
believe that anyone could have lasted long in the water.

The RNLI had only recently added a hovercraft to
the station and we were still trying to expand the crew and
build up experience. The conditions meant the hovercraft
was working at its operational limits, and of course some of
the crew had never even seen a dead body. Suddenly, they
found themselves entering what can only be described as a
sea of bodies.

Our volunteers worked non-stop for 22 hours in the
hope of finding more survivors, but it wasn't to be.

In the days that followed, Mr Guy got the crews and their wives
together to explain the long-term emotional effects of such
horrific sights.

I wanted them to understand why they were probably going
to wake up in the middle of the night shouting. I wasn't trying
to scramble their heads; just help them understand that this
would be a perfectly normal reaction. Likewise, if they had
repeated flashbacks, then they needed to see a doctor to talk
things through.

There were all sorts of rumours flying around, such as the
Chinese mafia being involved. For some crew, that translated
in their nightmares to people chasing them. This was a really
quite traumatic time for some of them and that is why the
camaraderie of the RNLI – the feeling that you're part of a
family – is so important. I believe it is our greatest strength.

Despite everything, the crew members all stayed together. We didn't lose a single one and that says something about both them and the organisation they serve.

Today Patricia Fisher is president of the Ladies Lifeboat Guild at Haslingden, Rossendale, Lancashire. She has spent years raising funds for the RNLI. But her earliest memories were forged on holiday in St Anne's between the wars in a childhood marked by a tragedy that happened years before she was born.

'I can remember going along the promenade of St Anne's and always standing to look at the statue. It always fascinated me. I didn't understand what it was about at the time, but I can remember once when we were on holiday, so long ago, we heard the maroon go off in the night. It made me think about what those lifeboat men must have gone through.'

As she grew up she learned that the statue was dedicated to local heroes. It made her determined to help lifeboat crews, which is why she became a fund-raiser.

'Courage like that and the dedication they give now deserves some support and they need that support. They are going out on a winter's night in a howling gale to rescue someone that they never knew and will never know again. They are risking their lives. When they get the shout they don't go and stand on the beach and say, had we better go tonight? There's no hesitation, they just go and do the job they are trained to do.

'That is why we need the money to train them to the highest standard and to provide them with state-of-the-art boats, the equipment and their clothing to make sure that they are as safe as they can be. We can't do anything less than that.'

Above: Port Erin and Port St Mary lifeboats assist a catamaran taking on water near Port St Mary.

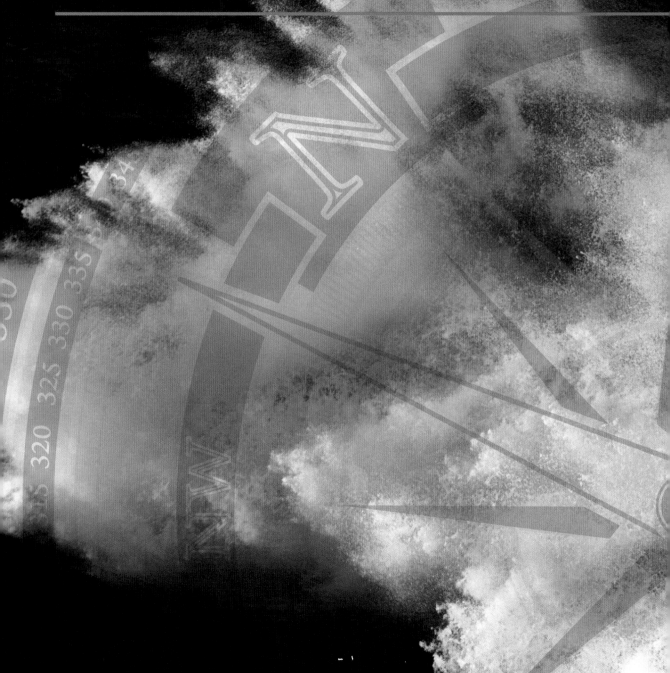

SCOTLAND

MALIN
HEBRIDES
FAEROES
FAIR ISLE
CROMARTY
FORTH

ts coast is remote and rocky, its weather rarely serene. There was little doubt in anyone's mind that, when the foundation stones of the RNLI lifeboat house were laid in Fraserburgh in 1858, a sorely needed service was being brought to the heart of a fishing community.

Saving lives had long been a preoccupation among local people. A lifeboat was in operation at Fraserburgh as early as 1806, one of the first in the British Isles, organised by the harbour commissioners, who claimed a sixpenny toll for every man entering the harbour by ship to pay for it.

Royal Navy Lieutenant Charles Bowen and a team of coastguards distinguished themselves there in 1827 by rescuing three men, two women and a child from the wreck of the *Rose*. The shore-based team used the Manby mortar to get a line to the *Rose* and, working waist deep in freezing water, helped bring the stranded ashore. Bowen was rewarded with a silver medal.

The harbour commissioners' second lifeboat had already been broken up, however, by the time the RNLI got to work. Fraserburgh became its first Scottish station.

With the unpredictable North Sea either licking or lashing at Fraserburgh's shores, the lifeboat was kept busy. But in the 20th century it was not its hectic schedule for which it was best remembered but the string of tragedies associated with its name. Thirteen men lost their lives in three separate incidents spread over half a century, leaving a community scarred by recurring grief.

The first occurred on 28 April 1919, when the lifeboat *Lady Rothes* was launched to assist a struggling Royal Navy vessel, *Eminent*, helpless after its engine failed in a gale. (Lady Rothes was a survivor of the *Titanic* disaster in 1912 and had both rowed and helped steer a lifeboat until it was picked up by the RMS *Carpathia*. Afterwards the able seaman in charge of the *Titanic* lifeboat, Thomas Jones, presented her with its brass nameplate as a token of his admiration of her behaviour under extreme duress. The RNLI lifeboat was donated by her father, Thomas Dyer-Edwardes, who named it after her.) The lifeboat had arrived in 1915 and was the first motorised one to operate at Fraserburgh.

Above: Fraserburgh lifeboat house – the first of the RNLI's Scottish stations.

A mighty wave upended the 42-foot lifeboat, which was almost immediately turned over by a second before it could right itself. Eleven of the crew survived by clinging to the upturned hull as it was swept to shore, but coxswain Andrew Noble and acting second coxswain Andrew Farquhar drowned. Noble was the veteran of numerous rescues and had won two silver medals from the RNLI for his bravery on previous occasions. Once he manipulated a lifeboat's broken rudder with his hand dangling outside the boat as he saved the crew of a trawler in the herring fleet. The crew of the *Eminent* were saved with the rocket apparatus set up on the rocky beach.

In 1953 it was the lifeboat *John and Charles Kennedy* that capsized in foul weather within sight of the town as she tried to escort fishing boats into the harbour. Coxswain Andrew Ritchie, George Duthie, Charles Tait senior, James Noble, John Crawford and John Buchan all died. The only survivor was Charles Tait junior, who was flung out of the boat and swept to the safety of the shore.

On 31 March that year, transport minister Alan Lennox-Boyd told Parliament what had happened:

Opposite: Portree Trent class lifeboat *Stanley Watson Barker*.

> The Fraserburgh lifeboat went out on the afternoon of Monday, 9th February to escort fishing vessels into the harbour. At the time a very heavy swell was running and as the lifeboat was approaching the harbour entrance on her third return journey a heavy sea lifted her stern into the air and broke amidships. Almost immediately a second sea struck the lifeboat on the starboard quarter, filling the cockpit and the space under the canopy. All the crew except the coxswain were swept forward against the engine controls under the canopy and the lifeboat capsized. One of the crew managed to escape from the lifeboat and swam ashore. The other six were drowned.
>
> While every step is taken to ensure the greatest possible safety for the crews that man the lifeboats round our coast, I am afraid we shall never altogether overcome the risks that necessarily attend heroic and gallant service of this nature. Fortunately, however, tragedies of this nature are very rare.

In the same year six lifeboat men, including two brothers, were lost at Arbroath, on the same Scottish coast, after their boat *Robert Lindsay* was overturned outside the harbour. In 1959 all eight crew of the Broughty Ferry lifeboat *Mona* died when it overturned. And Fraserburgh went on to defy Lennox-Boyd's statistical reckoning by experiencing a third disaster on 21 January 1970, when five crew members died in similarly atrocious weather.

The maroons went off at 7.35 a.m., calling the crew to the *Duchess of Kent* lifeboat. Toolworker James Buchan was on his way home, having just completed a night shift, and leapt aboard the boat as she passed the pier.

The weather was stormy, but that was nothing unusual for the lifeboat. She was going to the aid of a Danish fishing boat, the *Opal*, which was reportedly taking on water some 38 miles from the coast. Just after midday the lifeboat was escorting the *Opal*, but soon it was flipped over by a forceful wave.

The dead were coxswain John Stephen, the town's assistant harbourmaster; Fred Kirkness, the lifeboat's engineer; William Hadden,

Right: Spray on lens, thanks
to the North Berwick D class
inshore lifeboat.

a Customs and Excise officer; and two men – James and James Slessor – both named Buchan.

Survivor John Jackson Buchan was thrown clear and picked up by a nearby Russian trawler. The crew of the Russian vessel tried to right the lifeboat. Eventually, when it was recovered, four bodies were found trapped inside. The body of Fred Kirkness was never found. More than 10,000 people attended the men's funerals, including the Duke of Kent, the President of the RNLI. The tragedy left five widows and 15 children without fathers.

John Buchan became a taxi driver and died in 1999 without ever speaking publicly about what happened.

A subsequent court of inquiry stated: 'No vessel can be guaranteed to survive all possible sea conditions and this lifeboat was unfortunate to encounter a very large wave which overwhelmed her.'

The calamity occurred a year after eight lifeboat men died at Longhope, on the Orkneys, when the lifeboat *TGB* capsized. Coxswain Daniel Kirkpatrick was lost with his two sons, Daniel and John, while mechanic Robert Johnston died alongside his sons, Robert and James. The other crew members were James Swanson and Eric McFayyen. The disaster was a devastating blow to the small town on the island of Hoy. The litany of post-war lifeboat disasters was completed by the capsize of the Seaham lifeboat in 1962, costing a total of nine lives.

The principle of self-righting boats had been sacrificed for the sake of better handling at sea, with the approval of both the RNLI and its crews. But at what cost? It was impossible to tell if lives would have been saved with self-righting boats, but a seed of doubt had been planted about lifeboat design. Once again the spotlight turned to self-righting lifeboats and engineers tackled the concept with renewed vigour, restoring it to the 'must have' list on lifeboat design.

Above: Zac the sheepdog falls 100ft down a cliff then refuses to come out. He's caught in an inaccessible ridge that only a lifeboat can get near. One lifeboatwoman put ashore has the task to coax (then drag) him to safety.

One of the most dramatic tales of heroism and death linked to the lifeboat service in Scotland was a recent one that involved the lifeboat out of Lerwick, in the Shetland Islands, where the seas are busy with oil rigs and factory ships.

On 19 November 1997, the 3,600-ton refrigerated cargo ship *Green Lily* fell foul of challenging weather. Sea spray was riding high, as was the ship's bow. Then *Green Lily* developed engine trouble and was left floundering in a prevailing wind that would surely drive her to a serrated shore.

At first it was thought that tugs would provide the most practical answer to *Green Lily*'s problem, by lassoing her and pulling her to safety. But when a tow line could not be established it was time for the lifeboat and the coastguard helicopter to get involved.

On the advice of the lifeboat, *Green Lily*'s anchor was dropped, to put a brake on her drift towards the coast. As the lifeboat tried to come alongside to collect the 14 crew and its captain, it was lurching violently up and down, one moment below the freighter's deck and the next high above it. The risk of a collision matched the likelihood of *Green Lily* being smashed against the rocks. At one point the lifeboat was trapped by the angle of the big ship and only swift and determined throttle work by coxswain Hewitt Clark saved the lifeboat from being submerged.

By the time five men had come aboard, *Green Lily* was turning, leaving the lifeboat exposed to the pounding waves and howling winds. It pulled away, and the hovering helicopter was now the focus of the rescue. In little more than ten minutes, ten members of the crew were winched into the helicopter. All that remained was for winchman Billy Deacon, who had supervised operations from the deck, to be hoisted aboard and the drama would draw to a close. But before he could attach himself to the wire an enormous wave broke over the

WHILE TRAGEDY HAS HAUNTED SCOTTISH SHORES, IT IS MORE THAN MATCHED BY STORIES OF TRIUMPH

deck and swept him from sight. Almost simultaneously, the stern of *Green Lily* smacked into the rocks.

As the helicopter crew peered into the gloom for a glimpse of the orange overalls of their lost comrade, the dangling wire snagged in the ship's rigging. Only swift work by the winch operator in cutting the wire prevented the helicopter being downed.

Realising that the chances of Deacon surviving were negligible, Clark took the difficult decision to return to Lerwick with his passengers, although he returned immediately to the wreck to continue the search. Deacon's body wasn't found until the following day, seven miles distant.

Afterwards, Hewitt Clark was awarded the RNLI gold medal for gallantry along with the Maud Smith Award for the bravest act of life-saving in 1997. It was the pinnacle of a life-saving career in which Clark received a plethora of awards.

The RNLI saw it like this: 'Coxswain Clark demonstrated incredible skill in handling the lifeboat and taking her alongside the violently rolling casualty and rescued five men from the vessel in horrendous weather conditions.

'He made the decision to launch after it appeared that all other hope had gone: a tow line had parted, the helicopter could not work the casualty, and she was close to the rocky shore; there was no margin for error.

'Coxswain Clark manoeuvred the lifeboat in limited sea room, with 15-metre breaking seas and violent storm force 11 winds. When he finally drove the lifeboat clear with five survivors on board there was less than 200 metres to the shore.'

More importantly, perhaps, he ultimately gave 34 years' service in lifeboats and saved 319 lives.

While tragedy has haunted Scottish shores, it is more than matched by stories of triumph. At Fraserburgh's neighbouring station of Peterhead, for example, coxswain James Cameroon won two silver medals: one in 1916 for locating the wreck of a liner in pitch darkness and saving 74 people, the second the following year for rescuing 41 people from three ships, all wrecked in the same storm.

In 1940 the *Julia Park Barry of Glasgow*, Peterhead's lifeboat, recorded a busy day's work after it launched at 7 a.m. in severe

weather. She went first to the steamer SS *Lisbon* to rescue 30 crew men before arriving alongside the SS *Simonburn*, driven on rocks by harsh weather in the same vicinity.

When she was filled to capacity, the lifeboat landed passengers at Fraserburgh before returning to the *Simonburn* to collect the last 16 people aboard. It was then the turn of the SS *Baron Minto* to receive a visit. The ship had run aground, and 24 crew were liberated from her. Finally the SS *Alcora* needed help. Eventually the lifeboat returned to port at 4 p.m., having been at sea in shocking conditions for more than nine hours and having rescued more than 90 people.

In 2002 Bill Hall, who was among those rescued from the *Simonburn* that day 62 years earlier, returned to Peterhead to present the successors of that remarkable crew with a commemorative plaque.

When three men lay grievously injured on an oil tanker near Scapa Flow in 2006 after the forward deck where they were working was washed down by two enormous waves, the first response of the coastguard was to call on the men of the Longhope

Left: Oban Trent class all-weather lifeboat *Mora Edith Macdonald* towing the yacht *Bold Explorer*, which had suffered an engine fire.

lifeboat. However, it was soon apparent that the rough seas would make it impossible for the lifeboat to come alongside the Singaporean vessel *FR8 Venture*. The injured men also needed more medical attention than the lifeboat crew could offer.

Quickly the crew came up with an idea. They called on local doctor Christine Bradshaw to ask if she would help. Once she was aboard she was told about a plan to winch her from the lifeboat into a coastguard helicopter, which would then lower her on to the deck of the tanker. All this in a 15-metre swell created by force-12 winds. Before they embarked on the mission no one knew she had never been in a helicopter before, although she didn't let that faze her. 'Tell me what to do,' she said to the crew.

When the helicopter hovered above to winch Bradshaw aboard, the pilot and crew saw her making her way across the deck of the Tamar lifeboat on her hands and knees, to avoid being washed away.

From the helicopter Bradshaw could see that conditions would be no better aboard the tanker. 'As we approached the tanker from

Above: Dr Christine Bradshaw, who was awarded a bronze medal for her courage.

its stern, the whole of the deck was awash with water. I did wonder how on earth we were going to get down there.'

Despite the atrocious conditions she was successfully winched aboard, where she found one man dead and another dying. However, with her help, the third was stabilised and flown to hospital with neck and back injuries from which he eventually made a full recovery.

Bradshaw was awarded a bronze medal by the RNLI for her courage that day. More than that, the experience inspired her to join the crew.

In 2009 the crew of the Dunbar lifeboat *John Neville Taylor* set off in appalling weather after a Swedish yacht made a distress call. The *Ouhm* had been built by Jonas and Ingrid Akerblom for a round-the-world trip, but the first leg of it was marred by huge waves and a force-nine gale that threatened to drive them on to the Scottish cliffs in the middle of the night.

Even in the eyes of the lifeboat men it was a terrifying sea. Coxswain Gary Fairbairn said: 'I've never experienced a sea as big as that and as violent as that in all my days at sea. … this sea was fierce. One false move and it would have taken you. …I've never seen a sea like that and probably will never again, hopefully not anyway.'

He could still spare a thought for the people he was intent on saving. 'It must be like sitting in a washing machine for hours waiting for help to come.'

Stuart Pirie was one of the volunteers on the lifeboat that evening. Although a fisherman and an experienced lifeboat man, Pirie agreed: 'The weather conditions were terrible. I've been a fisherman for many years, I've been round Britain on lifeboats, and I've never seen weather like that before.'

'Abysmal' was how mechanic Kenny Peters described the weather that night. 'We knew we were going to be in for a rough ride.

Above: Three kids and their mum are caught on a rock by a fast turning tide. The RNLI Dunbar lifeboat makes two trips to rescue them and literally carry them to safety on a nearby shore.

We knew with the way the sea had been all day it was going to be a pretty horrendous night … it was one of them, we were just going to have to grin and bear it and get on with it. No question at all, the boat always goes to sea.

'It was the swell and then the wind on top of it. It was a sea I'd never been out in before, especially in a lifeboat. When you're on a 14-metre boat and you've got anything between 10- and 15-metre swells or waves coming at you it's not a nice view when you're looking out the window and you see what's coming towards you … but at the end of the day that's what we're here to do.'

The boat shuddered as it hit big waves and even rolled on to its side on a couple of occasions. Meanwhile the yacht was being continually swallowed from sight by the swell, and without its glowing mast light the lifeboat might never have found it.

When it became clear that towing the *Ouhm* to safety was out of the question, the crew persuaded the terrified Akerbloms to abandon their yacht. It took considerable skill to bring the lifeboat alongside the yacht without mowing it down. The lifeboat men hauled the couple aboard and headed for home.

Coxswain Fairbairn was given a bronze medal for his seamanship, while the rest of the crew were recognised for their bravery with certificates.

'Gary and his whole crew did an incredibly good and risky job when they picked us up, much more than you can expect anyone to do for you,' said Jonas Akerblom afterwards. To his relief the yacht was recovered the following day by the lifeboat from Arbroath.

Much later, crew member Brian Cleator identified another successful aspect of the mission. 'On the day the crew worked together extremely well. One thing that was obvious was that for any kind of team to work under extreme conditions we all have to look after each other, and that was one of the things that was very much in evidence … I think it's a testament to the amount of time that we do spend training and how close we are as a crew here.'

Besides contributing to its records of gallantry, Scotland has made other important contributions to life-saving in Britain. It was Scotsman George Lennox Watson (1851–1904) who pioneered a new style of lifeboat that helped increase the flexibility of the lifeboat service.

The son of a Glasgow doctor, Watson spent his childhood in awe of the immense ships built on the River Clyde and entranced by the graceful boats he saw moored on the estuary near the family's holiday home in Ayrshire. In his youth he served an apprenticeship with Clydeside shipbuilders Robert Napier & Son, but he already had the ambition to go it alone.

In 1873, aged only 22, Watson established the first yacht design business in the world, capitalising on his gift for design. Soon his reputation for excellence was well known and he attracted orders from some of the wealthiest clients of the era, including the Vanderbilts and the Rothschilds. It was Watson who drew the distinctive lines of HMY *Britannia,* the most successful racing yacht of all time, after a commission by King Edward VII when he was Prince of Wales.

His interests were not confined to luxury yachts, however. Watson was also intrigued by lifeboat design and the need for a resilient and serviceable boat to help save lives. In 1887 he became the chief consulting naval architect to the RNLI, and his design spawned the familiar Watson class of lifeboat. But this was not a self-righting type, which many associated with the RNLI felt was the first priority of design.

Yet, against expectation, it was popular with crews. At 38 feet in length and stabilised by water ballast tanks, it was quick to launch and durable at sea, where it could go further and deeper than previous lifeboats.

In 1897 Watson told the Parliamentary inquiry into the work of the RNLI: 'My feeling with regard to the self-righting boat is, in the case of the smaller pulling boat, certainly and possibly even in the case of the larger pulling boats too, that it would be unwise and unsafe to abandon the self-righting principle. With the large sailing boat I think

IT WAS WATSON WHO DREW THE DISTINCTIVE LINES OF HMY *BRITANNIA,* THE MOST SUCCESSFUL RACING YACHT OF ALL TIME, AFTER A COMMISSION BY KING EDWARD VII

Above: A Watson lifeboat
– robust and popular with
crews. Her designer,
George Lennox Watson,
also designed racing yachts.

we can get a better boat by abandoning the self-righting principle, but I would not risk it with the smaller boats.'

He was also keen to see motors used in lifeboats. Before his untimely death Watson designed 432 yachts, lifeboats and other vessels during a 32-year career, an output which averages one new build launched every three and a half weeks. His company maintained its association with the RNLI, with his successor James Rennie Barnett continuing ground-breaking work that brought petrol-driven engines to lifeboats. In August 1909 a long-distance trial proved that the motorised lifeboat was still a work in progress.

Three lifeboats headed out along the Thames with the aim of discovering which was the best model. One was a large Watson class sailing boat heading for Thurso, in the north of Scotland, the second a slightly smaller Watson boat with a 40-horsepower engine, bound for Stronsay in the Orkneys, and the third a self-righting lifeboat with a 30-horsepower engine, going to Stromness in the Orkneys.

Although official reports spoke glowingly of the engines, they

were in fact unreliable. News that they pulled in for repairs frequently after rough weather was suppressed. However, history has shown that this was the way ahead and improvements continued to be made. Eventually, in the middle of the 20th century, the petrol engine would give way to diesel power – more economic, less flammable – but not before motorised boats made a significant contribution to life-saving.

Another significant contribution to the saving of lives around Scottish shores came in the form of lighthouses. The history of the lighthouse is a long one – the idea of illuminating a rocky promontory with a beacon of fire goes back to ancient times. The case for illuminating the Scottish coast, with its 800 islands and 11,000 miles of mostly rocky shores, became pressing after fierce storms in the 1780s claimed scores of ships. The Northern Lighthouse Board was created by Act of Parliament in 1786 with the stated aim of building four lighthouses. The man who stepped up to the task was engineer Thomas Smith, who was responsible for Edinburgh's street lighting.

Smith married a third time to widow Jean Lillie Stevenson and became stepfather to her son Robert Stevenson (1772–1850). Stevenson had been brought up in poverty, but he taught himself the rudiments of engineering and was then taken under the wing of his stepfather. He became stepson, apprentice, business partner and eventually son-in-law to Smith, when he married Jean, Smith's daughter by a previous marriage.

Smith alone designed a number of lighthouses for the NLB, including those at Kinnaird Head, the Mull of Kintyre and North Ronaldsay. Together with Stevenson he built several lighthouses, among them Inch Keith and Start Point and was responsible for 13 lighthouse projects before his death.

Stevenson went on to become a noted engineer and the founder of a dynasty of lighthouse builders. His first major project remains

Above: Dunbar inshore lifeboat *Jimmy Miff* is called out to two surfers who have been caught out by the rip current at Belhaven Bay.

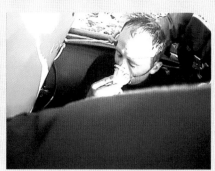

a monument to his expertise. The Bell Rock Lighthouse stands 11 miles off the east coast of Scotland. It's a white stone tower some 100 feet high, planted on a submerged sandstone reef. Since its completion in 1811 it has never required a major repair. Prior to its construction the rocky outcrop on which it is built claimed numerous ships down the centuries, when the only warning to seafarers was a monastery bell established by monks as close to the sea as they could get.

Basing his design on Cornwall's Eddystone lighthouse, Stevenson pondered the difficulties of both building offshore and keeping the lighthouse upright when it had perpetually 'wet feet'. The price tag, he believed, would be a mighty £42,685. His initial proposal was promptly dismissed by the NLB. Only after 491 men died when HMS *York* foundered on Bell Rock in 1804 did they look again at his plans.

Initially, the NLB turned to John Rennie, a favoured engineer of the era although not an expert in lighthouses. Rennie was responsible for the inclusion of an exaggerated curve at the lighthouse base, designed to better withstand waves. However, it was Stevenson that had daily control of the project – and work could only take place in the summer months for two hours at low tide. Indeed, Rennie visited the formidable lighthouse site only twice during the four years it took to finish.

The workforce enjoyed little by way of labour-saving devices and relied mostly on muscle power, assisted by primitive pulleys, to bring dovetailed granite blocks into position. At its base the lighthouse measures 42 feet in diameter, while its lantern housing is just 15 feet wide.

The ambitious Stevenson seems to have been determined to take credit for the completed lighthouse. Rennie was philosophical about his name being omitted in accounts of the lighthouse project, but one man who should have at least shared some of the limelight was Francis Watt, the site foreman. He devised lifting cranes for men and

HIS INITIAL PROPOSAL WAS PROMPTLY DISMISSED BY THE NLB. ONLY AFTER 491 MEN DIED WHEN HMS YORK FOUNDERED ON BELL ROCK IN 1804 DID THEY LOOK AGAIN AT HIS PLANS

building materials as well as the temporary barracks built on stilts to house the men working there.

From the moment on 1 February 1811 when the 24 oil lanterns were lit and began to blaze from the top of Bell Rock, the prospects for seafarers around Scottish shores were considerably brighter. And the completed project was considered a wonder of the age, proof that Scottish skills were indeed more accomplished than those in neighbouring England. Stevenson hired artist J. M. W. Turner to paint the Bell Rock, and he himself published a book detailing its construction. It was the first of 15 lighthouses constructed by Stevenson in his capacity as engineer for the NLB, a post he held between 1808 and 1842.

Stevenson's three sons, Alan, David and Thomas, all became lighthouse engineers too. Alan is best remembered for his work on the Skerryvore light, branded 'the noblest of all deep sea lighthouses'. Like Bell Rock, it was built miles offshore and on a difficult reef.

Brother David was even more prolific, involved in the building of 29 lighthouses. His most distinctive finished product was the brick-built lighthouse completed at Muckle Flugga, which he called 'an untried experiment in marine engineering'. It was finished with the help of Thomas in 1854.

Early ambitions fostered by Thomas to become a writer were greeted with horror by his father. In fact, Thomas went on to become a highly respected lighthouse builder, although now he is best known for being the father of writer Robert Louis Stevenson, who acknowledged the life-enhancing skills possessed by his family when he wrote: 'Whenever I smell salt water, I know I am not far from the works of my ancestors. The Bell Rock stands monument for my grandfather, the Skerryvore for my Uncle Alan, and when the lights come on at sundown along the shores of Scotland, I am proud to think they burn more brightly for the genius of my father.'

His cousins, David and Charles, were also noted lighthouse designers, and between them the Stevensons wreathed Scotland with light. Indeed, the author who gave us *Treasure Island* was under considerable expectation to follow the family line himself, until he showed little aptitude for engineering.

Robert Stevenson and his sons brought the job of lighthouse keeper into being, and in so doing they brought to an end the once-flourishing

Opposite: Queensferry Atlantic 75 inshore lifeboat *Donald and Ethel Macrae* patrolling the waters around the Forth Rail Bridge (behind).

business of wrecking by hard-hearted coastal dwellers. They also did much to improve the quality of light emanating from the top of the towers. The number of lives saved since the inception of modern lighthouses is inestimable.

Scottish scientist Sir David Brewster (1781–1868) helped when he perfected his experiments with refracted light. Although French physicist Augustin Fresnel took greater credit for developing a lens that increased the power of light, it was Brewster who, as early as 1820, campaigned for such lenses to be incorporated into lighthouses.

The Stevensons' signposts of the sea are still used today by mariners. Even lifeboat men whose local knowledge is second to none can become disorientated in big seas. Nor are experienced lifeboat men afraid to ask for advice when extra information could mean the difference between life and death.

On 21 June 2006, a yacht in the Round Britain race got into difficulties off the Hebrides. Said yachtsman Huib Swets: 'We were beating against wind all the way. Suddenly there was a huge bang, like a car crash. I think the ship pitch-poled.'

His first concern was for his co-pilot, who had been covered with mattresses and cabin equipment when the vessel somersaulted. Then he rang the coastguard, who sounded the alarm.

The nearest lifeboat was at Barra Island, and coxswain Donald MacLeod ran straight to the boat without even pausing to assess the sea. 'I didn't get a chance to see conditions before we left the station,' he admitted later. But he had hurried in case the casualty was forced into the treacherous Sound of Barra. Indeed, his best hope of intercepting the yacht was to go through the Sound himself.

There are three acknowledged routes through the Sound. Now MacLeod did find time to call his father Rod to get a shore-side assessment of the best option for the lifeboat. But the surf was foaming as far as the eye could see. 'It didn't matter which way they went, it was all a mass of white, all the way across,' said Rod. The lifeboat made a hasty but nerve-racking voyage across the Sound and found the yacht shipping water but still making headway under its own power. Together the boats returned through the Sound of Sandray, a far safer option.

Above: A crew member at St Abbs lifeboat station in the early twentieth century.

MacLeod was awarded a bronze medal for his quick actions that day. The rescue came just 24 hours after two other yachts were rescued by the Barra lifeboat in similarly high seas.

Barra Island lifeboat station is one of 14 in Scotland to have a Severn class lifeboat, the largest boat in the RNLI fleet. In service since 1995, the lifeboat is big, weighing 42 tonnes, but nonetheless nimble, with propellers and rudders set into tunnels in the hull. Inside it is lavishly equipped with modern communications, electronic charts, oxygen and all manner of kit designed to combat emergencies at sea. Like the Tamar, the Severn carries a daughter boat that's suited to operations in the rocky inlets that typify Scotland's shores. It travels at a speed of 25 knots in small to moderate seas.

Intent on producing future heroes, the RNLI invests a lot of its resources into projects that encourage younger people to join. Louise Graham, from Loch Ness, became the first graduate of the RNLI Future Crew Scheme, which aims to recruit, retain and rehearse future members.

Only 18 years of age, Louise has already performed on two rescue missions. Accidents happen frequently in the loch, so she is not short of practice. 'Call-outs to people getting into trouble whilst swimming are common, and the worst are canoeists who get stuck, sometimes when they are submerged. They are the most serious because it's touch and go if we get there in time.'

Above: Watson motor class *Margaret*. George Watson's successor in his company, James Rennie Barnett, continued his pioneering work to make motorised lifeboats a reality.

295 300 305 310 31 315

FASTNET
SHANNON
ROCKALL
MALIN
IRISH SEA
LUNDY

When the construction of a lighthouse was too expensive or beyond the expertise of engineers, an alternative means of warning shipping about hidden perils was to use a lightship riding at anchor. First experiments with a lightship at the mouth of the Thames were so successful that Trinity House, the authority in charge of lighthouses, took out a patent claiming the idea as its own. In Ireland, the Commissioners of Irish Lights (CIL) is the lighthouse authority.

A lightship, as its name suggests, has a beacon high in its masts to warn passing shipping of shallows or rocks. Initially this was an oil lamp, but later it was fixed lamps with Fresnel lenses. By 1861 there were 34 lightships around the English coast and four off Ireland.

Early lightships were manned, and the eight crew were sailors for all seasons, facing autumn gales and winter storms. The stoutly made vessels were held in place by one hefty mushroom-shaped anchor attached to the ship with an iron cable, and each carried a spare in case the first was fouled.

It was a stray lightship that triggered one of the most famous rescues in Irish history. The Daunt Rock lightship was placed to alert craft about the hazards of Cork harbour. Like other lightships, it was distinctive for its bright red body with its name *Comet* in white letters picked out on the side.

On 10 February 1936, a powerful storm swilled around the Irish coast, strong enough to break the cable which held the lightship to its anchor. Forty years previously, this lightship's predecessor *Puffin* had been lost on just such a night, along with all eight crew. Now *Comet*'s crew knew that they too were in extreme danger. A maroon was fired, visible from the nearby town of Cobh, and then they began battling to deploy the spare anchor.

Later a crew member related the drama. 'On Monday night the wind went mad in its fury, the seas continually pounded us and, indeed, it looked as if we were lost. At one o'clock on Tuesday morning our cable … parted and we were being blown towards those hated rocks of Robert's Cove. We worked like demons to run out our second cable … Those 20 minutes taken to perform this operation seemed like an eternity. We made another attempt and you can guess the joy we experienced as we felt the anchor grip the bottom and check our progress to destruction.'

Opposite: A crew member is winched up to a helicopter from a Trent class all-weather lifeboat.

Of course, the weather wasn't much better in Ballycotton, where the lifeboat was based, as RNLI honorary secretary Robert Mahony testified in his report. 'Stones, a ton in weight, were being torn from the quay and flung about like sugar lumps. I spent most of the night near the lifeboat house watching the terrible destruction that the wind and waves were doing. Twice I was spun round and nearly flung on my face. At three on the Tuesday morning I went to bed but not to sleep. I was out again shortly after seven and found that the coxswain and the other men had been up all night trying to secure his motorboat. They had succeeded in launching a boat, got a rope to the motorboat and secured her. It was at that moment after this long night of anxiety that the call for the lifeboat came.'

It seemed unlikely the lifeboat *Mary Stanford* would even get out of the harbour, let alone to the site of the drama. But with coxswain Patrick Sliney grimly steering into steep waves a monumental rescue began to unfold.

It took some time to locate the lightship and, when it was found, two other ships were standing by, including the destroyer HMS *Tenedos*. The *Mary Stanford* joined the vigil for three hours before returning to Cobh. When the lifeboat returned the following day the destroyer departed. With the crew unwilling to abandon the lightship, as it would be a threat to shipping, the lifeboat stood by for a further 25 hours.

As fuel ran low she returned to Cobh once more to find additional help in the shape of *Isolda*, an Irish Lights vessel. However, when the lights of the *Comet* were extinguished by a huge wave that in turn pushed the vessel towards the rocks, Sliney knew it was time to act.

More than a dozen times, he took the lifeboat alongside to liberate the lightship crew. Six of the men summoned sufficient courage to jump into the lifeboat as it halted momentarily to ride the waves. Two were frozen with fear and would have to be pulled from their perch on the deck rails. Reluctantly Sliney sent his own men forward to stand by to grab them, desperately hoping they would not fall victim to the waves themselves. As the lifeboat passed close by the *Comet* for a last time, the pair were dragged to safety by men of the lifeboat.

The trauma of the night wasn't over, though. One man from the lightship – who had been tossed and thrown around for the past three days with no certainty of survival – became hysterical and had to be pinned down by lifeboat crew.

In the RNLI Journal *The Lifeboat* the rescue was dubbed 'one of the most exhausting and courageous in the history of the lifeboat service'. The lifeboat crew had been at sea for nearly 50 hours and awake for more than three days. Sliney was awarded the gold RNLI medal for his courage that night, with silver awards going to his brother, motor mechanic Thomas Sliney, and second coxswain John Walsh. Sliney's other brother John and son William, who were in the crew that night, received bronze medals, as did Michael and Thomas Walsh.

Today lightships are no longer manned. Those that are placed in dangerous channels are solar powered, although most have been replaced by light buoys.

Apart from the names Sliney and Walsh, another looms large in Ireland's life-saving history. Henry Alexander Hamilton (1820–1901) was a magistrate, a supporter of the church and, for 46 years, the honorary secretary of the RNLI lifeboat based at Skerries, north of Dublin. Some administrative figures chose to use their influence over rescues from the safety of the shore. Hamilton was not among them and, moreover, he embodied a positive 'can do' attitude that turned apparently hopeless causes into triumphs over adversity.

Left: Rowing lifeboat at Skerries station.

His concern with life-saving began on 20 December 1853, when the brig *Agnes* was driven ashore on the Leinster coast in fearful weather, at a point too distant for the nearest oared lifeboat to help. Hamilton was among the onlookers who tried to launch a small boat to rescue its crew, but they were beaten back by the bad weather.

Hamilton then came up with an idea that seemed almost laughable. If someone took the next train to Dublin to issue an alert, the lifeboat from there could be loaded aboard an empty wagon for the return rail journey. The plan was adopted, the lifeboat duly arrived the following day at a local station, and Hamilton with five others launched it immediately. At first the wind and waves once again proved too strong, but after several hours the storm abated and in darkness the lifeboat came alongside the brig to bring its master and two seamen to safety. Two others had drowned.

For this Hamilton was awarded a silver medal. More crucially, he resolved to build a lifeboat house at Skerries to prevent tragedies like this happening again in the full gaze of the town. He also campaigned for a new lifeboat, and by the end of 1854 it had arrived.

Hamilton didn't need a lifeboat when he spotted a woman in difficulties in the water south of Dublin in the summer of 1858. He dived in to save her, and in gratitude she donated £300 to the RNLI. After she wrote to the Institution with the donation, Hamilton received a second silver medal.

In the same year an Austrian coal-carrying ship, *Tregiste*, ran into difficulties on 17 November between Lambay Island and the mainland, a treacherous channel even in calm conditions. And this night the weather was poor. Once again Hamilton approached the rescue with a characteristic creativity. He organised horses to transport the lifeboat south from Skerries to the beach nearest the disabled vessel, some five miles distant.

Then he launched, into intolerable conditions, and for two hours lifeboat and crew battled to reach the casualty, with both vessels at risk from lunging waves. Finally, Hamilton realised that the lifeboat was not going to reach its target. With the crew exhausted, it retreated to the nearest shore. But Hamilton did not give up hope for those aboard the *Tregiste*. From the safety of a coastguard cottage he and his men kept a vigil.

And finally, at about 3 a.m. the following morning, they were rewarded as a lull in the weather gave them an opportunity to launch. It still took two and a half hours to reach the *Tregiste*. But when they arrived they found 13 crew all alive. With daring seamanship the lifeboat came around the stern of the ship and the men were hauled aboard, including two who had been severely injured when the mast was cut down in an attempt to stop the *Tregiste* drifting on to rocks. It was a five-hour operation that left the men involved drained but elated.

Hamilton was rewarded for his patience and determination with the Institution's gold medal. As it happened, the anchor of the

Tregiste prevented the ship from being smashed on the rocks and she was towed to safety soon afterwards.

In the years that followed storms were a regular occurrence around the Irish coast, but some were worse than others. A few were so bad they became the stuff of folklore.

On Christmas Eve 1895, Ireland was paralysed with grief after a lifeboat disaster that claimed 15 lives. It happened when the steamship *Palme* from Finland got into difficulties in a storm that was later dubbed 'the most severe of the century'. Waves were so fierce they crashed over the top of the lighthouse at the end of Dun Loaghaire's east pier. Although the captain had been heading for the shelter of Dublin's harbour, the ship was being taken towards rocks.

A comparatively new lifeboat, *Civil Service Number Seven*, manned by 15 local men, responded to the *Palme*'s distress rockets, but before it reached the ship the lifeboat was flipped over by a mighty wave. Frantic efforts by the sailors of the *Palme* to rescue them came to nothing when the ship's lifeboat was also smashed.

A second lifeboat left Dun Loaghaire – then known as Kingstown – and also capsized. Fortunately it righted itself, and the cold, wet crew managed to climb back aboard and the boat returned to shore. Another lifeboat and two tugs were also forced to turn back.

Christmas Day passed with the bodies of lifeboat men being collected from the shores and the traumatised population watching breathlessly as the *Palme* endured endless punishment from the weather.

It was the following day before the steamship *Tearaght* reached the *Palme* and took off the 17 crew and the captain, his wife and their child. *Tearaght's* Captain Thomas McCombie won a gold medal from the RNLI for this feat of seamanship.

The 15 men who died were coxswain Alexander Williams, his father and former coxswain Henry Williams, John Baker, John

Above: RNLI Crosshaven lifeboat rescuing a very lucky kitesurfer. He was spotted in the failing light of a July evening drifting out of Cork Harbour after he was unable to raise his kite out of the water.

Right: Dun Laoghaire Trent class lifeboat *Anna Livia*. In 2010 Dun Laoghaire crews launched 50 times, bringing 60 people to safety.

Bartley, Edward Crowe, brothers Thomas and William Dunphy, Francis McDonald, Edward Murphy, Patrick Power, James Ryan, brothers George and Francis Saunders, Edward Shannon and Henry Underhill. The disaster made widows of 13 women and left 36 children fatherless.

Above: Naming Ceremony of Watson motor-class lifeboat *Dunleary II* in Dun Laoghaire in 1938.

Lifeboats from Ireland along with several from the south-west of England were all called into action in 1979, when the Fastnet yacht race was decimated by a major and unseasonal storm.

The Fastnet race is one of five that make up the Admiral's Cup competition, attracting the elite of the sport. Every year competitors set off from Cowes on the Isle of Wight, heading for the Fastnet Rock off the coast of Ireland. Once they have rounded the rock it is full sail ahead for the finishing line at Plymouth to complete a 605-mile course.

In 1979 the race began on a sunny day in calm waters. But a storm was brewing, catching most of the sailors unawares. The result was nothing short of a catastrophe. By the end of 14 August, 25 of the 306 yachts taking part were sunk or wrecked and 15 lives had been lost.

WITH 329 PEOPLE
DEAD AFTER A
BOMB EXPLODED
ABOARD, IT
WAS THE
WORLD'S WORST
TERRORIST
ATROCITY PRIOR
TO THE ATTACKS
IN THE USA ON 11
SEPTEMBER 2001

A further six people died in other craft at sea in the vicinity. In total 69 yachts did not finish the race. To their assistance went one of the most comprehensive rescue missions ever mounted in the UK.

Three Royal Navy vessels, a number of its helicopters, the entire Irish navy, a Dutch frigate, RAF Nimrods and 13 lifeboats joined forces to scour a storm-lashed ocean looking for survivors, whose onboard equipment was considerably inferior to that available today.

Framed certificates marking the contribution made by the Irish lifeboats were sent to coxswains and crews at Ballycotton, Courtmacsherry, Dunmore East and Baltimore. They spent hours at sea riding tumultuous waves trying to locate and save terrified and exhausted yachtsmen.

There was one unexpected result of the Fastnet race that's still in evidence today. One crew rescued by the RNLI from a sinking boat was so impressed with its professionalism and grateful for the timely arrival of the lifeboat that its members resolved to help with fund-raising. Bedraggled and battered, they never forgot the restorative powers of the first hot drink they had in the safe confines of the lifeboat. The result was the creation of Lifeboat Tea, sold in RNLI shops and supermarkets everywhere to raise funds for the charity.

On the 25th anniversary of the Fastnet disaster a plaque was presented to Coxswain Kieran Cotter and members of the Baltimore lifeboat with a citation that reads: 'The heroic work of Coxswain Christy Collins and crew of the Baltimore Lifeboat, *The Robert*, who rescued the crew of the *Regardless* and *Marionette* and towed both yachts to Baltimore is acknowledged as an extraordinary feat of seamanship conducted during the storm in which the 15 Fastnet race competitors perished.'

In 1985 the coxswain and crew of the station at Valentia received a framed letter of thanks after recovering five bodies from an Air India Boeing 747 which crashed some 115 miles offshore on 23 June. With 329 people dead after a bomb exploded aboard, it was the world's worst terrorist atrocity in terms of number of lives lost prior to the attacks in the USA on 11 September 2001.

The most recent medal winner in Ireland is lifeboat mechanic Anthony Chambers, who swam into a cave to rescue two teenage boys trapped by a rising tide.

On 5 August 2009, the Belfast coastguard called for both lifeboats at Portrush to launch, after the boys went missing near a rocky outcrop. Voices had been heard from the sea caves in Castlerock Downhill, which were now rapidly filling with water. A shore-based cliff rescue team were unable to reach them.

Hopes that the inshore lifeboat would be able to enter the cave were initially dashed by the turbulence of the swell. One crew member, Karl O'Neill, tried to swim from the boat to the boys, but his progress was hampered by his lifejacket.

Chambers immediately adjusted his lifejacket to let some of the air out. It meant he could swim more efficiently through the water. He then swam into the cave and felt his way to the back, where he found Matthew Forsythe and Reece Sufferin, cold and scared. He had taken with him a spare helmet and life jacket, which he now strapped to Matthew. Together they swam out of the cave, bobbing like corks in the waves and kicking in unison.

Opposite: Portrush Trent class lifeboat *Dora Foster Mcdougall*, which was one of the boats called out to rescue two boys trapped by a rising tide in 2009.

Left: A medivac in process, with a Courtmacsherry Harbour lifeboat crew assisting a fishing vessel.

'A few times we had to use our feet to kick ourselves away from the rocks because the surges were always pushing us across to the far side of the cave,' explained Chambers.

They reached the inshore boat, and he prepared to set off again under the crew's eagle eye. They knew he was now tiring. Fortunately, as the swell began to die down with the approach of high tide, the deft RNLI boat could make its way into the mouth of the cave, where Chambers and Sufferin were picked up. The boys were taken to the all-weather lifeboat which had been standing by, and from there were winched aboard an Irish coastguard helicopter which took them to hospital to be treated for hypothermia.

'It wasn't like swimming in a swimming pool,' said Sufferin later. 'It was a lot tougher and we wouldn't have been able to do it without Anthony pulling us along.'

Pamela Forsythe, who had raised the alarm after her son Matthew and his friend failed to return to the beach, said: 'Anthony saved them and we owe everything to him. He is one brave man.' Chambers was awarded the bronze medal, while O'Neill and helmsman Gerard Bradley received letters of thanks.

There appeared to be little hope for two young men when their boat sank off the shores of Belderrig on 31 October 2010. Having taken a huge swell on board, their boat almost immediately capsized and only a series of fortunate events coupled with the expertise of the RNLI crew from Ballyglass saved them.

Coxswain John Gaughran, known as JT, was part of the crew sent out, and he was stunned at how lucky they were. 'It was unbelievable really. They had sunk at one o'clock that day. The two lads, 18 and 22, were thrown into the water. The 18-year-old lad could swim whilst the 22-year-old could not. Incredibly, moments after the boat sank, a life ring from their boat appeared next to

Above: A speedboat sank so quickly it left its two crew, who luckily were wearing lifejackets, in the water. The Irish Lights vessel, the *Grainne Uaile*, arrived at the scene and took them on board its small boat. A Galway RNLI lifeboat arrived and transferred the two men onto the lifeboat and provided first aid.

Overleaf: Baltimore Tyne class lifeboat *Hilda Jarret* at full speed – 18 knots.

them, which is very unusual due to the big swells being churned up by the ocean.

'Then, the life raft appeared next to them, which was just as miraculous. However, it was trapped within its casing. Fortunately, one of the boys had a rusty key in his pocket and sawed through the strap that was keeping the raft from inflating.'

When on the life raft, they followed emergency guidelines to the letter, crawling into plastic sacks to keep themselves warm. They were in the ocean for ten long, cold hours.

The RNLI were alerted to the situation by John Walsh, a volunteer crew member, after he was told that the vessel had not returned to Portulin when expected. He immediately called the coastguard. 'It was dark when we went out, and we knew they had been out in the water for a long time, but we had no idea they were on an inflatable raft.'

Coxswain Gaughran began to worry after a couple of search routes proved unsuccessful. Then, remarkably, they found the boys, after a rescue helicopter had spotted them and communicated their position to the lifeboat, which was nearby. Considering the vastness of the area they were searching and the lack of visibility, the two boys counted themselves very lucky. 'It was amazing that they appeared right in front of us,' said Gaughran.

Back in 1989, Belmullet did not have a lifeboat. But that year the harrowing experience of a family with young children who got into trouble provided the impetus for change. 'We could hear our neighbours in trouble out on the sea,' said Gaughran. 'They had gone to check on their lobster pots with strong winds and stormy conditions promised.'

The family had intended to get back before the storm, but it hit them before they headed for land. To make matters worse, the engine had failed and they were drifting dangerously towards the rocks as they desperately worked to fix the problem.

'We picked up their radio messages but we were powerless to help. By some miracle, just before they hit the rocks, the engine started again and they were able to scrape back to shore.'

The narrow escape awakened the people of Belmullet to the importance of having a lifeboat nearby. 'The next lifeboat north of us was 95 miles, and the next one south of us was 90 miles. From then on we wanted to make sure that there was a lifeboat in our community to help in events such as these.'

For a small community in a remote area of Ireland, Gaughran believes, the RNLI provides welcome security for families who have loved ones working at sea. 'The importance of the RNLI for Belmullet is that the community depend on having a lifeboat in their area. It makes everybody feel better that no matter what conditions, we are there to help in emergencies. It is a huge relief to families, many of whom depend on making an income from the ocean.'

Wicklow, one of the 43 lifeboat stations in Ireland, was taken over by the RNLI in 1857, when the life-saving craft was a 30-foot rowing boat. Since then there have been boathouses on several sites, not least because one was washed away by the sea.

In 1917 the town's lifeboat men risked their lives to save three men in a life raft that drifted to the centre of a minefield.

Today Wicklow has both a Tyne class lifeboat and an inshore lifeboat. The *Annie Blaker* has been on station at Wicklow since 1989 and is launched via a slipway. Accordingly, the propellers are fully protected within her steel hull. Like other RNLI boats she self-rights, thanks to inflatable bags that are activated if the lifeboat keels over beyond 90 degrees. Her top speed is 18 knots. The Tyne class carries a small unpowered daughter boat that can be paddled or veered on a rope into more inaccessible areas.

Wicklow lifeboat takes her name from the late Anna Lydia Blaker, who generously bequeathed to the RNLI a large donation which partly funded the building of the lifeboat.

The 'D' class inshore lifeboat is called the *Sheringham Shantymen*. On station at Wicklow since 2007, it was funded by the Norfolk folk group Sheringham Shantymen.

THE FUTURE

Writing in the 1860s, coxswain James Gilbert of Tynemouth reflected on the lifeboat man's lot. 'I venture to say that the loss of life, which I for one deeply deplore, out of thousands of men that man [lifeboats] is wonderfully small and at the same time we must remember they are only boats.'

The boats he had in mind were wooden, oar-powered and open to the elements. Today's RNLI fleet is a world away from such rudimentary craft; from the impressive Severn class to the agile inshore lifeboat, it is run through with bells and whistles that would probably render Coxswain Gilbert speechless. These professional and highly refined boats are a major asset when it comes to saving lives. Nor is the story over as regards lifeboat design.

In 2013, after a quarter of a century of service, the existing Mersey class of lifeboat will be replaced by the Shannon, a new breed that's been honed with considerable care by the RNLI over several years. A review by the RNLI throughout the 1990s revealed that a 21st-century life-saving service needed its major boats, large and small, to be capable of 25 knots in order to meet its obligation of providing a rescue up to 100 nautical miles out to sea. Designers knew that this quick-moving replacement boat would have to be diminutive like the Mersey class – capable of just 17 knots – to suit its prospective lifeboat stations, yet still robust enough to survive high seas.

The imperatives that guide the RNLI – such as safety and value for money – didn't change during the design process. Technology, meanwhile, was advancing almost daily. It was the job of the Technical department of the RNLI to distil all the variables into the best possible sea-going option.

Instantly RNLI designers investigated a new way of powering lifeboats. Previously, propellers were favoured, but these needed

Opposite: The new, improved hull of the FCB2. These more powerful and more manoeuvrable lifeboats are expected to be in service in 2013.

Overleaf: The FCB2 prototype, which is designed to replace the Mersey class lifeboat. It will be the first RNLI all-weather lifeboat to use water jets instead of propellers.

plenty of protection or they could be fouled. So engineers experimented with water jets buried inside the hull. Although water jet technology is not new in the marine industry, the E class on the Thames is the only lifeboat to use it until now. This means the Shannon can be driven clean out of the water without risking its most essential components, saving valuable moments when there is a casualty aboard.

The Shannon will also go further than its predecessor, with a range of 200 miles (with a 10 per cent fuel reserve) compared with the Mersey's 140 miles. It means the RNLI can comfortably fulfil its obligation to attend emergencies up to 100 miles from the coast of the UK and Ireland.

Inside, the Shannon shares with the Tamar class a sophisticated Systems Information Management System, or SIMS. This calibrates data from every part of the lifeboat in an easy-to-use format. Steve Austen, head of engineering support at the RNLI, explains why it is so important. 'It keeps bums on seats. The crew are safest when they are strapped in. With SIMS they can access all the information they really need to run the boat from their seats.'

Moreover, while the technology is cutting edge it is also simple to understand. 'It presents information in a user-friendly and intuitive way. We had to recognise that most of our crews go in lifeboats once every few weeks. If one of those times is at 3 a.m. you want them to snap into the shout without worrying about how to interpret the information presented to them.'

Although it looks the same as the SIMS on the Tamar, in use since 2006, the black boxes that operate the systems aboard the Shannon are more advanced and are better able to accept modifications. 'We are future-proofing the equipment,' explains Austen.

The Shannon, made of a composite material consisting of glass and some carbon fibre, can operate safely in 16-metre seas, although it won't reach its fastest speeds in waves of that height and velocity.

'Sea-going capabilities had to be as good as the Severn, Trent and Tamar classes, but the new lifeboat needed to be a lot lighter, which was a challenge,' says Austen. 'It needed to be robust and light so that we could use more available weight operationally for things like kit, extra fuel, a full crew and survivors.'

The key lay in the design of the hull, and that's been subject to a long trial period. RNLI engineers came up with their own plans but needed to be sure they were the best available. As a result, six lifeboat models were built for sea-going trials. One had a copy of the RNLI-designed hull, while the rest were designs drawn from across the globe. Indeed, some were already tried and tested and working successfully on full-sized boats. These were no ordinary model boats, though. On board they had cameras as well as complex electronic measuring gear that could work out the effects of acceleration, roll and pitch and balance.

Ultimately, despite the high standard of competition, the in-house design was picked to go forward for production as it proved to have the best overall performance.

There's a good reason why the 47-strong Technical department at the RNLI delivers. A closeness exists between crew and designers that leads to an almost instinctive understanding of what's required. Engineers like Austen have all spent hours in the company of lifeboat crews on open water to discover more about the onboard challenges.

Inside the Shannon there's a high-spec seat for crew members. 'We set about designing a seat that would completely isolate the crews from the effects of acceleration that sometimes cause injury,' says Austen. 'We ended up with a suspended seat, with a big spring and a big damper that absorbs all of the impact. It greatly reduces the potential for injury as the result of a big slam, when the boat hits a wave. It doesn't matter how well you drive the boat in the pitch darkness, you don't always know what is coming towards you.'

The Shannon also has a new-style tractor to launch it. It's different from the familiar agricultural-style tractor both in appearance and capability. This one can drive swiftly into seawater to launch the boat. If it happened to get stuck in the sand it could be immersed in a nine-metre tide and still emerge with its electronics in good order. With the new tractor the number of people needed for a beach launch will be reduced from six to two.

With the creation of the Shannon class the RNLI were keen to make a smaller boat compete with its bigger brothers in terms of efficiency, speed and durability. Yet they also had one eye on cost. Historically the operational life of RNLI boats is around 25 years. Now, thanks to the durable materials used in their construction, the RNLI is looking at ways of doubling that lifespan to 50 years. Studies are already underway to identify which parts of the boat will last longest – and conversely which will need replacing soonest. The aim is to target maintenance where it is most needed, and a replacement programme will be led by the condition of fixtures and fittings rather than the calendar. Accordingly the design of the Shannon lends itself to an easy re-fit. 'We believe we can save around £¾ million a year by better understanding the condition of the equipment rather than the fixed, calendar-based approach we've had until now,' says Austen.

Although the manufacture of components is contracted out, boat-building is now completed in-house. The RNLI bought a boat-building company in Lymington, Hampshire, in 2009 to ensure a security of supply. Once again, close communication between engineers and boat-builders has helped to save money as the builders come up with ideas of their own to improve and even speed up the manufacturing process.

HISTORICALLY THE OPERATIONAL LIFE OF RNLI BOATS IS AROUND 25 YEARS. NOW, THANKS TO THE DURABLE MATERIALS USED IN THEIR CONSTRUCTION, THE RNLI IS LOOKING AT WAYS OF DOUBLING THAT LIFESPAN

Opposite: The capsize pool in the Sea Survival Centre at the Lifeboat College.

Overleaf: Sheringham Atlantic 85 class lifeboat *The Oddfellows* following her naming ceremony.

There's a new-style life jacket being rolled out by the RNLI as well. As Austen explains: 'Life jacket design is currently 15 years old. In that time industry has moved on and the shape of people has changed as well. As a population we are getting bigger. If we look at the range of people who are in the RNLI we must cater for various sizes and shapes. The kit has got to be comfortable and fit for purpose for everyone.'

The result is a life jacket that's more buoyant than before, that far exceeds international safety standards and that's specifically designed for use in search and rescue operations. It is not made out of a new material; rather the constituent parts fit together differently and more efficiently.

The Shannon and the new life jackets which will be on board are a reflection of how the RNLI must respond to an evolving task. Long ago, the vast majority of call-outs were in the winter months and a result of bad weather. Today about three-quarters of the emergencies dealt with by the RNLI occur in the summer months, especially August. That's because leisure craft are now more numerous than merchant ships and fishing vessels.

Each lifeboat station in Britain has the craft and equipment deemed best suited to it, and the RNLI keep the changing coast under constant review, so that the most appropriate lifeboat is provided for every location. New marinas and shifting sand bars can alter the complexion of the life-saving landscape.

Once the lifeboat was called out when witnesses on shore saw a ship in difficulty. Today the process is more complex – but also far quicker. A distress call may be made by telephone using emergency numbers or via ship's radio. All ships and some leisure vessels carry emergency beacons which dispatch a radio signal when activated.

When a call for help has been received, HM Coastguard, the Irish Coastguard or the Channel Islands Coastguard decide how to

ONCE THE LIFEBOAT WAS CALLED OUT WHEN WITNESSES ON SHORE SAW A SHIP IN DIFFICULTY. TODAY THE PROCESS IS MORE COMPLEX – BUT ALSO FAR QUICKER

respond. There are the options of a helicopter, a lifeboat and mud or cliff rescue teams. If a lifeboat is needed, then the coastguard needs to ask for its launch.

Through an RNLI-owned paging system an alert is sent to the lifeboat operations manager or deputy launch authority. Once agreement is given to launch, the crew and shorecrew are called to the station by a second 'page'. Crew members keep their pagers close, so they are ready to respond in an instant.

When they arrive at the station the crew must kit up in protective clothing. Those on the all-weather lifeboats wear yellow waterproof trousers and jacket with matching wellies. The crew of the inshore boats have a dry suit and yellow wellies. Lifejackets and helmets are mandatory for both. Lifeboat shorecrew get to work while the crew are getting their gear on.

On average, an inshore lifeboat is launched in seven minutes and an all-weather lifeboat is off the blocks in 12 minutes, from a mooring, down a slipway or from a beach carriage launch.

Once aboard, the crew are in contact with the coastguard about the unfolding drama so everyone has an idea of what lies ahead. The coxswain also passes back the identity of the crew aboard, each of whom is known by a number rather than a name to avoid confusion when those with the same surname are together at sea. Some rescues take a matter of moments, while others can take hours. Communication with the coastguard and other craft in the vicinity is pivotal for speed.

When the operation is finished and the boat is back at the lifeboat station, it must be washed down and cleaned. Equipment is checked and items are replaced when necessary. The fuel tank is refilled, so the lifeboat is ready for the next emergency, when the procedure swings into action all over again.

Above: Primary school pupils from Temple Park Junior School in South Shields join RNLI lifeguards on Sandhaven beach to learn how to stay safe in the surf.

INDEX

82, 172, *188–9*, 191, 192; inshore (ILB) 5, 52, 54, *59*, *61*, *92–3*, 110, *133*, *158–9*, 171, *172*, 191, *200–1*, *216*, 235, 236, 238, 240, 251; invention of 22–6; managed by local committee 26, 28; Mersey class *49*, 52, *68–9*, 78, 82, *96–7*, *179*, 240, 244; motorised 45, 47, 48, 82, 213; Norfolk class 29, 32, 65–6, 82–3, *103*; petrol-driven 47, 83, 100, 164, 213–14; rigid inflatable boats (RIBs) 82; sail 65, 82; self-righting 9, 24, 28, 43, 54, 64, 65–6, 70, 92, 98, 120, 124, 132, 157, 179, 181–2, 202–3, 212–13, 238; Severn class *34–5*, *94–5*, *122–3*, 219, 240, 244, *245*; Shannon class 82, 240, *241*, *242–3*, 244, *245*, 247, 250; steam 146, 158; Suffolk class 29, 32, 65–6, 82–3, *103*; Systems Information Management System (SIMS) 244; Tamar class *84*, *121*, 150, 209, 219, 244; technology in 240, 244, *245*; Trent class *23*, *50*, 54, *198*, *204*, *208*, *223*, *230–1*, *235*, 244; tubular 154–5, *154*, *156*, 157; Tyne class *84*, *85*, *115*, 238; Watson class *135*, 142, 164, 212, 213, *213*, *219*, *232*; women help launch *42*, 45
lighthouses 11, 19, 32, 33, 36, 90, 128, 214–18, 222, 229

lightships 11, 222, 225–6
Lincolnshire Poacher 68–9, 78
Lisbon, SS 208
Lizard 128–9, *129*
Lord Southborough 105–6, *105*
Louisa 127, 128
Louisa Heartwell 73
Lovelock, Victor 'Danny' 91
Lowestoft 65, 66, 73
Lukin, Lionel 22, 23, 25, 26
Lymington 88, *92–3*, 247
Lynmouth 125, *125*, *126*, 127, 128
Lytham 65, 155, 178–9, *180–1*, 182

M

Macara, Charles 182–4, 186
McCombie, Captain Thomas 229
MacDonald, Rod 150, *150*
MacLeod, Donald 218–19
MacLeod, Rod 218
Madron, James 142
Mahony, Robert 225
Manby, George 58, 60–2
Manby mortar 58, 60–2, 196
Manchester Unity of Oddfellows 67
Marchioness 110
Margaret 219
Margate 103, 105, *105*, 106, 107
Mariner's Friend 145
Marionette 233
Mark Lane No. 3 66, 70, 71
Mary Stanford 95, 98–9, *99*, 225
Maynard, Kevin 114–15, 117
Mexico 178, 179, 181–3
Minna 29

Minnie Moon 129
Moelfre Bay 166–7, 170, 171
Mona 199
Monte Nevoso 74
Mora Edith Macdonald 208
Morecambe Bay 82, 187, *188–9*, 191–3
Moreton, Captain Henry 'Mick' 135
Morgan 154, 157
Morris, Jeff 52
Mount Ida 74
Mumbles, The 162–4, 166
Munt, Moses 91
Nafsiporos 167, 170
National Institution for the Preservation of Life from Shipwreck: barometers, buys for lifeboat stations 10; financial support for crew 9–10, 75; financing of 9, 10, 37–8; foundation of 6, 8–9; lobbies for benefit of seafarers 10–11; new ideas, keeps pace with 9, 10; silver gallantry medals 37; supporters 9; *see also* RNLI

N

New Brighton 82, 158, 161
Newcastle 23, 48, 77
Newquay *133*, *171*
Noble, Andrew 197
North Berwick *200–1*
North Britain 120
Northumberland, Rear-Admiral Algernon Percy, 4th Duke of 38, 64, 154, 187

O

O'Neill, Karl 235, 236
Oddfellows B-818, The 59

Opal 199
Orchard, William 147
Original, The 24, 25–6
Orkneys 202, 213–14
Ouhm 210–11
Owen, William 158, 161
Owens, Evan 167, 171

P

Pace 121, 124
Padstow *121*, 145–7, *148–9*, 150, 161
Palme 229
Parker, Edward 105, 106–7
Peake, James 65, 120
Penlee 134, 135, 138, *140–1*, 141
Penzance 120–1
Percy Garon II 82
Peregrine, SS 83–5
Perry, Frank 90
Peter Bond 191
Peterborough Beer Festival IV 82
Peterhead 205, 208
Peters, Kenny 210–11
Pirie, Stuart 210
Plenty, William 32
Port Eynon 161–2
Port St Mary 5, *190*
Porthcawl *160*
Porthleven 129
Portrush *234*, 235
Prichard Frederick Gainer 128
Princess Mary 147, 150
Providence 37–8
Prudential 104–5
Pryce, Simon 145
Pym, Richard Elsworthy 28

R

Ramsgate 22, 103, 104, 155
Redcar 26, 28, 29, *30–1*
Regardless 233
Regina 146
Rennie, John 215–16
Revi 77–8
Rhyl 65, *154*, 157, *157*,

CREDITS

All pictures © the RNLI except for: p.41 © The Sutcliffe Gallery, Whitby; p.135 © Lalouette Photographers; pp.148–9 © Studio St Ives

The RNLI would like to thank the following photographers who have supplied pictures for the book:

Dave Kneale; Chris North; Adrian Don; Nigel Millard; Andrew McAlea; Tom Collins; MC Major; RNLI Zetland Museum; Peter Bentley; Sgt. Rick Brewell ABIPP; Doug Jackson; Ray Brownlie; Chris Taylor; Steve Medcalf; Clifford Hicks; Nicholas Leach; Mike Irving; Rick Tomlinson; Sam Robbins; Hayley Beddons; Janie Airey; Andrew Filipinski; Chris Slack; Steve Guscott; Carl Wilson; Robin Goodlad; Stephen Jones; Emyr Rhys Williams; Peter Sykes; Nathan Williams; Martin Fish; Matthew Gibbons; John Watt; Hamish Campbell; David Branigan, Oceansport; Kelly Allen; Peter Booton

60 PER CENT – RNLI INCOME FROM
RNLI INCOME FROM FUND-RAISING
LIFEBOAT DESIGN IN 2010 £64.2 M
PER CENT – THE NUMBER OF RNL
4,600 – THE NUMBER OF VOLUNTEER
OF VOLUNTEER SHORE CREW AND
NUMBER OF LIVES SAVED SINCE 18
STATIONS IN THE UNITED KINGDOM
– THE NUMBER OF OPERATIONAL
LIFEBOAT LAUNCHES IN 2010 8,313
IN 2010 309 – THE NUMBER OF LIVE
OF A D CLASS INSHORE LIFEBOAT £
TAMAR CLASS ALL-WEATHER LIFEB
TRAINING A LIFEBOAT CREW MEMBE
BINOCULARS £85 – THE COST OF A
THE NUMBER OF UK BEACHES WITH
LIFEGUARDS ON PATROL IN THE SU
OF INCIDENTS DEALT WITH BY LIFE
OF LIVES SAVED BY LIFEGUARDS I
TRAINING A LIFEGUARD 22 – THE AV
EACH DAY IN 2010 £42 – THE COST O